Joshua's Long Day
@
American Tectonic Plate Movements

Atlantis Deluge @ Joshua's Long Day

notionpress.com

Joshua's Long Day
@
American Tectonic Plate Movements

Atlantis Deluge @ Joshua's Long Day

Anipe Steeven K.V. Premajyothi

notionpress.com

Notion Press

Old No. 38, New No. 6

McNichols Road, Chetpet

Chennai - 600 031

First Published by Notion Press 2016

ISBN 978-93-5206-944-6

Dedication

This book is lovingly dedicated to my wife
Smt. A. VIJAYA KUMARI

Who has been walking with me; serving the Lord with me; always praying and encouraging me in my efforts.

Contents

Preface

I am very glad to introduce this book to you at this time of confusion and turmoil. Generally I search for the Biblical issues by the help of God's spirit. While I was searching for a physical evidence for the Joshua's Long Day in the history of mankind, I got the evidence as I believed it was a historical fact. When I was searching major geological incidents in the history of earth the Atlantis story got my attention. Day and night I searched for evidences of Atlantis existence and its time of existence on the earth. I thrilled to know that many authors not supported the idea of Atlantis deluge in 9500 years before the time of Plato. Moreover I picked up a phrase 'Atlantis deluge in single day and night,' it increased my enthusiasm about how it was deluged in that little time. And I came to know that the first king of Atlantis was a Nephilim (Anakim).

As I have written about Nephilims in my first title 'Paradise Found' and I have much knowledge about their origin and their behavior through many books. In Genesis 6:4, there is this one phrase 'nephilims existed afterward...' This was became a key to unlock the mystery about Joshua's Long Day. The books written by many authors helped me a lot to arrive to a solution to this fact and answer to historical speculations about this issue for many centuries.

So there was link between 'Atlantis deluges in single day and night' and 'Sun stood still for about a day.' This link was revealed through this book with help of graphics.

I apologize to all the readers as I wrote this book in very simple language as I am not an expert in English. One thing I can tell that this book can be understood by every individual in this world. I am happy to release this book as a global book because Joshua's Long Day affected entire globe in the Old Testament times. How these incidents linked was explained in a straight way. So I request every reader to spread this news to your friends through social networks.

I am thankful to my family for their support, the churches for their prayers and Notion Press team for their friendly approach in publishing this book.

Anipe Steven Premajyothi
victorprem.vpc@gmail.com
9963181200

PRAISE THE LORD

Chapter 1

Creator and His Creation

God, the Creator, with His mighty power and glory created Heaven and the Earth. We know well that the earth is a tiny part of the universe and is the most beautiful and pristine planet of the solar system. We can see "In the beginning – God" is a phrase to reckon with in the Genesis, which brings us to wonder about God and where He came from. He always existed. Some still find it hard to believe in the existence of God and the acts are done by Him from the beginning. We should remember that "the secret things belong unto the LORD, our God: but those things which are revealed belong unto us and to our children forever" (Deu 29:29). The dawn of the nineteenth-century man exploring the infinite space at any cost by spending millions of dollars without an end to it. But how long did we traverse in these 100 years? The only end of the solar system we have been able to touch with space machines, as per the recent newspaper reports, is our space vehicle reaching one end of this huge expansive solar system. Every educated person is aware of the vastness of our universe and man is the sole intelligent and capable being to explore the infinite creation with his finite mind!

The Bible puts forward clarity about God's omnipotent power. For it is only here that we can learn from the following scriptures:

Psalms 135: 5-7 NKJV

5. For I know that the Lord is great, And our Lord is above all Gods.

6. Whatever the Lord pleases He does, in heaven and earth, in the seas and all deep places.

7. He causes the vapors to ascend from the ends of the earth; he makes lightning for the rain.

He brings the wind out of His treasuries.

And also in Isaiah 40: 15-18

15. Behold, the nations are as a drop in a bucket, And are counted the small dust on the scales; Look, He lifts up the isles as a very little thing

16. To whom then will you lien God? Or what likeness will you compare to Him?

When we think about the earth, every day we walk, touch, live on it, and we don't know much about the inner structure of the earth. If we study the inner structure of the earth, we certainly marvel at it, because it was omnipotent God's creation. Main parts of the earth are 1) Crust 2) Mantle and 3) Core.

GRAPHICS in Page no: 120 (Which Shows Interior Earth Structure and Cone-Shaped Graphic)

We can see the earth as a spherical ball in space, but it has an incredible inner structure in it. Its formation is divided into Lithosphere, asthenospheric mantle, outer core and the inner core. Even in this age of science and technology, geologists hardly knew about the scientifically-proven facts of the inner structure of the earth. Many assumptions have been made about the inner and outer cores of the earth. With the imaging systems available today, multiple facts about the inner earth have come to light. We are proud of our scientists and geologists who have been able to unearth the wisdom of the creation of God. Bible states that God, the Creator, laid the foundations of the earth.

"Where were you when I laid the earth's foundation? Tell me, if you have an understanding." Job 38:4.

And also in Romans 11:33 "Oh, the depth of the riches of the wisdom and knowledge of God! How unsearchable his judgments and his paths beyond tracing out!" (NIV).

When we think of the tectonic plates of the earth and their structure and movements we should remember the Omnipotent God, who made this wonderful planet and everything in it. Tectonic Plates are a fragment of geological science which developed in the early sixties and today we have steady and sufficient information about these tectonic plates of the earth. Geologists have made it possible for us to know more about the creation of Omnipotent God.

Omnipotent God:

God of this creation is all pervasive and all-knowing; He is the Beginning and the End; He is Almighty even though Satan rules over this age; the ultimate power over every situation is in the hands of God. The authority and the ownership were given to Adam in the Garden of Eden as he has to subdue the earth from Satan's habitation. Because of his fall, the authority was given to Satan "the God of this Age" (2 Corinth 4:4).

Ultimately, God reigns in this world and accomplishes His plans. Cross was the alternate plan of God when man failed Him in subduing the earth. As far as the free-willed man is concerned, the plan of God seems to be a failure, but if we can see the end, God is the Victor. With His Omnipotent power, God created the earth and all in it. When we think about the layers of the earth, we understand the Omnipotent power of God. By His word, God gathered the earth (land mass) in Genesis. In the Genesis account, we learned about the gathering of water to one place. God brought up - the tectonic plates (continents) shifted, automatically the waters reached lowest places and the oceans formed at the beginning. Several tectonic plates of the earth assembled by the power of the Word of God thus, forming the dryland.

"God called the dryland Earth, and the gathering of the waters He called seas, and God saw that it was good." (Genesis 1:10 KJV)

God of the Bible is the Omnipotent God, and He was the only Creator of Earth and Heaven. The scientists have been trying to understand this vast universe and exploring human limitations. In fact, even in this fast-paced technological world, the man had limited knowledge about the inner parts and the functions of earth.

By God's grace, 1960s onwards, the geologists succeeded in understanding the tectonic plate movement of the earth. Many books were written, and extensive research was undertaken to understand the tectonic plate movements in this century.

Bible discourses in the Genesis 18:14, "Is anything too difficult for the LORD? At the appointed time I will return to you, at this time next year, and Sarah will have a son."

Further, the Bible says, "And looking at them Jesus said to them, 'With people this is impossible, but with God all things are possible"(NASB).

Luke 1:37 says, "For nothing will be impossible with God" (NASB).

Dryland Formed – Genesis Account

Apostle Peter, in his epistle, wrote that by waters God moved (tectonic plates) the earth and made it appear as a dryland in the beginning. God created the earth with a combination of certain tectonic plates and this wonderful planet suspended in space like a spherical ball.

"For they deliberately overlook this fact, that the heavens existed long ago, and the earth was formed out water and through water by the word of God" (II Peter 3:15).

Tectonic plate movements are the latest geological discovery regarding the structure of the earth and the pattern of their movement. We know the earth was created by God and the inner and outer structure belongs to God's plan. These tectonic plates were on earth and part of the earth as per God's plan.

Please continue to read this book to know why the author is putting forward these facts and reasoning. The author is going to prove that some tectonic plates of the earth at a certain place was moved apart, and some other plates moved into the inner earth. There was an unavoidable link between the Deluge of Atlantis and the occurrence of Joshua's Long Day in the Old Testament Bible days. It has been an intriguing fact which is revealed. Here God's Omnipotent power is evident in physical, spiritual matters of mankind and earth. Genesis account reveals that in a single day the dryland and the oceans were formed. At the time of Joshua, God showed the same power to perform a miracle in the land of Canaan by hearing an urgent appeal of His servant. The author is going to explain the acts of God in the light of geological occurrences clearly, and the mystery of Joshua's Long Day and the Deluge of Atlantis are revealed with certain evidence. So please be patient to read every chapter of this book.

To understand this book, we have to feed our spirits with the power of God. So please read the following scriptures which would reveal the power of God.

"God is all-powerful" (Genesis 17:1) indicates that He can do anything He intends.

"It is He who made the earth by His power, who established the world by His wisdom, and by His understanding stretched out heavens" (Jeremiah 10:12).

Job declared, "I know that you can do all things and that no purpose of yours can be thwarted" (Job 42:2).

God is Almighty. By hearing Moses prayer, God performed a miracle of making way in the Red Sea as the waters stand just like a wall. Can we explain this scientifically? No. But this miracle happened, and we have many pieces of evidence for this miracle. God brought streams of water from a rock in the wilderness. How can it be possible to bring rivers of water to satisfy thirsty people of about two million at a time?

When we think about God's act of bringing Global Flood and demise of Atlantis in one day and night, we may misunderstand His acts but behind the scenes, there were unavoidable reasons for all these facts. From the beginning, God was not happy on the acts of Nephilim, who were the offsprings of illegal marriages between sons of God and daughters of the Man.

My other title *Paradise Found* has clearly explained why loving God deluged the earth with a global flood in Noah's days. Nephilim penetrated the society in those days and as per the Bible, the effect continued later as well. The offsprings of illegal marriages before the global flood were called as Nephilim and after the flood, they were called as Anakim. Sometimes these words were used interchangeably. Both were the offsprings of illegal marriages between Sons of God (angels) and Daughters of Men. There was an increasing support to the appearing of angels in human form. Bible supported these aspects many times. The people of Sodom and Gomorrah tried to molest the angels physically in Lot's house. The angels bolted themselves in the house. In the Old Testament, Jacob wrestled with an angel all through the night. The angel asked Jacob to let him in as day broke. In the *Book of Judges,* the man called Manoah saw the angel and spoke to him assuming he was a man. Therefore, one can trace multiple incidents of angels appearing like a man. But fallen angels morphed into human form against the will of God with the intention of polluting the human race. This was the main reason God took a wrathful decision of exterminating them from the face of the earth. As Atlantis concerned the Anakim in that period propagated wrong belief system, and they tried to subdue every nation turning every lower tribe into slaves incorporating pride and arrogance as primary behaviors.

Let us discuss the existence of Nephilim after the global flood and their continued existence in the next chapter.

Chapter 2

Existence of Nephilim After Global Flood

Origin of Nephilim

According to Genesis 6:4, we come across Nephilim. The Nephilim, product of Sons of God, intermarry with the Daughters of Man, the great giants (man of renown), 'the fallen ones' came into existence as a hybrid generation. It was once claimed that mating of the Sons of God and the Daughters of Adam resulted in the origin of the Nephilim race on earth.

The Sons of God accepted the same as the Angels took a decision against the will of God under Lucifer's direction; took wives for them and married the daughters of Adam. God viewed this seriously and through operation of the flood, God removed all Nephilim from the face of the earth. This was clearly explained in my other book *Paradise Found*. Why Lucifer encouraged this act of marrying daughters of man was because he intended to pollute the human race completely to place obstacles in the incarnation of Jesus Christ. God wanted to preserve the seed of man to send Messiah to save mankind completely from the influence of the enemy. Noah was a righteous man in God's sight. God preserved the family of Noah and initiated the human race, yet again, to flourish on this earth. In the post-flood era, the descendants of Noah increased in a rapid way with God's blessings at the foot of Mount Ararat.

(Quote: Dr Michael Eaton, Preaching Through the Bible Genesis 1-11 Hadlow, Tonbridge, Sovereign World Trust, 1997, 123)

A distinct Bible teacher, Dr Michael Eaton, wrote:

"A third view is that this refers to something very mysterious which took place in the world of angels "Sons of God" refers to angels. This is the view I think is right. The phrase "Sons of God" in Hebrew refers to angels (See Job 1:6, 21: 38:7 which refers to the time when there were no human beings, Ps 29:1; 89:6).

This event is mentioned in I Peter 3:19-20, 2 Peter 2:4 and Jude 6 where it is interpreted as referring to angels.

It might be asked: Can this happen? Can angels marry people? Remember this point: Angels may look like men (Gen 18:2,8; 19:1,5). They may be dressed like men; they may eat and drink. As discussed before, the men of Sodom tried to molest angels physically."

Can Angels take the form of a man? The materiality of angelic beings seems to be an age-old belief. We know from Genesis there was the angel with whom Jacob wrestled. The author of the book of Genesis called him as a man; even somewhere the Bible reveals that he was an angel. The 'angel' said to Jacob: "Let me go, for the day breakout: And he said, I will not let thee go, except thou bless me."

The angels who came to Lot's house at Sodom had to be bolted indoors of Lot's house to protect them from an intended sexual assault by the people of Sodom. Sodomites were the ones who wanted to know the angels (Genesis 19:5). In the *Book of Judges*, Manoah offered to cook dinner for his guest and the appeared angels presumed to be ordinary men. (Judges 13:2 - 16). Here, Manoah did not realize that he was the angel of the Lord.

We can find an intriguing statement in Genesis 6:4, "The Nephilim were on the earth in these days, and also afterward when the sons of God came into the daughters of man, and they bore children to them. These were the mighty men who were of old, the men of renown" (ESV).

Here we should observe the phrase "and also afterward." This means after the global flood the revolt of angelic beings continued under the direction of the Lucifer, the Satan. We know that the Noah's Flood happened around 3000 BC. After the end of the Flood, the descendants of Noah thought of constructing a tower which saved them from any flood of the same measure. They did not remember God's promise or His rainbow which assured them for not sending a global flood again. Therefore, they began to construct a tower in the plain of Babylon. During construction, their languages changed and they were unable to continue the project in anyway. The construction stopped, and people began to migrate away from Babel. The author believes that at the same time descendants of Noah might have reached the new continent Atlantis, which was situated against the Pillars of Hercules. The epic written by some authors tell us that the people of Atlantis were fair skinned, and their women were enviously beautiful. The angelic beings once again intermarried the daughters of man on the land of Atlantis as in Genesis 6:4. It was stated that the Nephilim existed after the flood also. They gave birth to the founders of the nation of Atlantis for which Plato, the great philosopher narrated the story of Atlantis!

(Quote: Atlantis - The Mystery Unraveled by Jurgen Spanuth, The Citadel Press, Section One, The Historical Basis of the Atlantis Legend, 1956)

"Plato, the great Greek philosopher, and thinker (429–347 BC) has recorded for us the legend of Atlantis at two different places in his writings – in the Dialogue of Timeous and of Critias of the origin and substance of the legend Plato tell us this:

Solon, Legislator and one of the Seven Sages of Greece (640–559 BC), made a journey to Egypt seeking knowledge of ancient times. He visited the city of Sais, whose priests had an unequaled reputation for their intimate knowledge of ancient history. There he was received with great kindness and showered with honor. The priests were only too happy to pass on to him the information they had extracted from their vast collection of papyrus and ancient texts.

The disorders and sufferings of those times were believed to have been caused by gigantic natural catastrophes of universal impact. The Egyptian priest reminded Solon of the Greek legend of Phaethon, Son of Helios, and God of the sun, who entered his father's sun chariot; unable to keep to his father's course, he burned or scorched many countries of the earth in the terrific heat of his passing. Eventually, Zeus hurled Phaethon from the sky with a stroke of lighting and extinguished the great fires with floods and rainstorms."

The author Jurgen Spanuth recorded the incident, and he mentioned the sun chariot and the God of Sun that scorched the countries of the earth. Why did this author mention about the severe heat that prevailed during this catastrophe? It is learned that the flames and fires traveled up to the land of Libya and even to Egypt during this catastrophe of Atlantis. When the tectonic plates opened at the junctions of North America and Eurasian plates, the flames and lava came out with tremendous force unequaled to any modern volcanic eruptions or catastrophes. So when the Atlantis deluged in the Atlantic Ocean, the devastation was not comparable to any incident, it may be equal to the destruction caused by thousands of nuclear bombs. This type of devastation was possible only when the tectonic plates opened, and the lava burst out with incredible speed and force.

Atlas as a Nephilim?

Nephilim (from the *Atlantis Encyclopedia* by Frank Joseph)

Described in the Old Testament as a fallen race of giants, they ruled the world before the Great Flood, which obliterated their power. Their descendants, the Emim, "a people great, and many, and tall" (Deuteronomy 2:11), were also known as the Rephaim or Anakim, who perpetuated pre-deluge religious practices atop a sacred mountain, Seir. The Nephilim appeared to have been late fourth millennium BC Atlanteans.

Atlas

(Graphic: - Page no: 121 Of Atlas Who is Bearing a Sphere)

"It is said that Atlas was the chief monarch of the ancient Atlantic nation. He ruled from its island capital. The forefather of the Atlantis nation was a giant called Atlas. From this name, the land was called as Atlantis and Ocean together were called as the Atlantic Ocean. We can see him in the graphic as a giant who is supporting the sphere of heavens from his shoulders.

It is written that after the division of land on earth Poseidon became the ruler of Atlantis. Then he settled his offspring he had once begotten with mortal women. Atlas was the oldest son of Poseidon and Cleito, the first king of Atlantis."

In ancient days even after the global flood, the Nephilim (Anak) race came into existence by the intermarrying of 'Sons of God' and women of Adamic race. A demon prince ruled over a region (watch over) on earth was supported by the Book of Daniel. In Daniel 10: 12-13 (KJV), Daniel was visited by an angel who had been opposed by 'The Prince of Persia,' may be the fallen angel that controlled the Persian region. "Then said unto me, 'Fear not, Daniel: for from the first day that thou didst set then the heart to understand,' and to chasten thyself before thy God, thy words were heard, and I come for thy words."

So from the above scriptures and historical facts, the Atlantis was the real place ruled by the giants during their existence. There was a land of Atlantis and flourished as an empire after the global flood.

Atlantis is a beautiful land and great ancient empire the dimension of which is as big as Asia Minor and Libya combined. It is said that roofs of Atlantis temples were made of gold, and the kingdom was tremendously wealthy. Many minerals were available in that land, and they knew how to mine them. They learned crafting of alloy metals and because of these metal weapons and strength of the Giants made them possible to build colossal buildings and great pyramids and canals in the rocky area. There were many types of wild animals and sprawling green pastures to sustain them. It is said that their main occupation and the source of income was mining. They mined gold and unbelievable amounts of brass and copper. They knew how to build a bridge and architecture and plantations.

Regarding their government each of the ten kings ruled over his section as per the laws of the land. They assembled once in every five years and discussed general rules and laws. Nobody could break the laws framed in the nation. The sea-god Poseidon was worshiped. People frequently indulged in bull fights and offerings. The author believes that they built big temples or pyramids to know the way to their land. When they saw the giant construction from a distance, they thanked their Gods for bringing them back safely from their voyages.

Now we must explore the civilizations that flourished in the vicinity of Atlantis. Before the Deluge of Atlantis, North and South American continents were in different locations. The author will discuss this subject in another chapter which deals with Tectonic Plate movement. Please be patient to continue reading, as it will reward you with a mystery which buried under the waters of Atlantic Ocean. The ambiguity of the subject was mainly because there was no scope of excavation and uncover the facts about the land of Atlantis. That was the primary reason why multiple books were written about Atlantis and many claiming its existence on every part of the earth and even on Mars. But in an attempt to analyze the data available, by using God's spirit the mysteries can be understood by the society in a right way. The books written so far were the stepping stones to arrive right destination in today's time. The author has gone through all claims and picked up one phrase 'one terrible day and night.' This was the authors 'key' to open iron door of age-old mystery.

Let us read the definitions of required words in the Atlantis Encyclopedia by Frank Joseph. The notes given by this author helps us to understand the origin of these words used in the ancient text of Atlantis:

(The_Atlantis_Encyclopedia.pdf)

Atlantology (Atlantis Encyclopedia by Frank Joseph)

The study of all aspects related to the civilization of Atlantis; also refers to a large body of literature (an estimated 2,500 books and published papers) describing Atlantis. It calls upon many related disciplines, including archeology, archaeoastronomy, comparative mythology, genetics, anthropology, geology, volcanology, oceanography, linguistics, nautical construction, navigation and more.

Atlanteans

The central figure in the story of Atlantis is the chief monarch of the Atlantean Empire, ruling from its island capital. Atlas was the founder of astrology astronomy (there being made no original distinction between the two disciplines), depicted as a bearded Titan or giant supporting the sphere of the heavens on his shoulders, as he crouches on one knee. He, thus, became a symbol and national emblem for the Atlanteans and their devotion to the celestial sciences. In Sanskrit, *atl* means "to support or uphold." In parallel, mythic descriptions of Atlas are revealing. His father, in the non-Platonic version, was Lapetus, also a Titan, who was regarded as the Father of Mankind. After his defeat by the Olympians, Lapetus was buried under a mountainous island to prevent his escape, suggesting the sunken island and punishment meted out to Atlantis by the Gods, as described in Plato's account. Clymene was the mother of Atlas, who was a sea-nymph personifying Asia Minor. Interestingly, "Atlas" is the name of a mountain in Asia Minor (Modern Turkey) near Catal Huyuk, which, at 9,000 years old, is among the most ancient cities on earth.

Thus, in Atlas's parentage are represented the Far West of the Atlantic islands (Lapetus) and the eastern extent of Atlantean influence (Anatolia) in Clymene. Her parents were Tythys, "the Lovely Queen of the Sea," and Oceanus, the oldest Titan, known as the "Outer Sea," or the Atlantic Ocean itself—all of which underscore Atlas's oceanic identity, contrary to some scholars who confine him to Morocco and the Atlas Mountains. Plato's version of Atlas' descent makes Poseidon, the sea-god, his father, and Kleito, the native girl of the ocean isle, his mother. These discrepancies are unimportant because the significance of myth does not lie in its consistency, but in its power to describe. Titan's transformation into a mountain took place after he fetched the Golden Apples for Heracles, who temporarily took Atlas's place in supporting the sky. He had been condemned to this singular position as punishment for his leading role in the Titanomachy, an antediluvian struggle between Gods and giants for mastery of the world. But Perseus, Heracles' companion, took pity on Atlas and turned him into a mountain of stone by showing him the Gorgon Medusa's severed head. This largely Hellenistic myth from early classic or late pre-classic times added peculiarly Greek elements, which clouded a far older tradition. Even so, certain details of the original survive in the Titanomachy, the Atlanteans' bid for world conquest, of which the depredations of the so-called "Sea Peoples" against Pharaoh Ramses III's *Egypt*, Homer's *Iliad*, and Plato's *Atlanto-Athenian War* were but various campaigns of the same conflict. According to Sumerian scholar Neil Zimmerer, Atlas was indigenously known in West Africa, where he was remembered as "the king of Atlantis, and fled when the island sank into the sea. He established a new kingdom in Mauretania."

When we observe the ancient picture of 'Atlas,' the picture narrated as holding up the heavens upon his shoulders, we should observe that it was not just the earth in context but the entire universe that one needs to bring into the purview of study. This type of thought pattern was not possible for the Bronze Age people. The evil spirits behind the Atlanteans that propagated were the originators of the entire universe. It was the challenge to God, and this thought pattern influenced all nations in that unscientific era. This type of belief might have been prevalent in those days. So the people of Atlantis practiced the king's worship and bull offerings practiced to the kings who were the Nephilim in this land of plentitude. This is one of the reasons for God, who took this severe punishment upon the people of Atlantis and at the same time God removed the other batch of Anakim by hearing the prayers of Joshua on that day in 1405. Please remember when the author mentioned the year 1405 BC for the Deluge of Atlantis, if and only if it was the correct year of Joshua's Long Day. If we can arrive at the correct date for the Joshua's Long Day with our super computers, that date will be the exact date of Atlantis deluge. This has been proven through this book.

The author believes that the land of Atlantis completely spoiled their ways and followed wrong beliefs in an attempt to conquer all other nations back in time. The creator of the universe, observed all these practices and with his foreknowing knowledge, determined to eradicate this race from the face of the earth. And He also decided to begin a race that will propagate His laws to the future generations of the earth. The kingdom of the evil spirit backing was terminated, and the race of Israelites proliferated on this earth. This was the decision of Almighty God. No one could suggest to God Almighty.

(Graphic: -Page no: 122 Map Showing Atlantis and Plate Junctions)

Let us discuss some cultures of different people that flourished in the vicinity of Atlantis.

Mayans

Let us take some definitions from the Atlantis Encyclopedia by Frank Joseph:

Aztecs

The Nahuatl-speaking people were the ones who established their capital, Tenochtitlan, at the present location of Mexico City, in 1325 AD Over the next two centuries, they rose through military aggression to become the dominant power in pre-Conquest Middle America. Although their civilization was an inheritance from other Mesoamerican cultures that preceded them, the Aztecs preserved abundant and obvious references to Atlantis in their mythic traditions. Despite the millennia that separated them from that mother civilization, their royal ancestry, though not entirely unmixed with native blood, could still trace itself back to the arrival of Quetzalcoatl, the "Feathered Serpent," an Atlantean culture-bearer.

Aztecatl

The Aztecs themselves drew their national identity from this term, which means, "Man of Watery (that is, sunken) Aztlan," the Aztec name for Atlantis.

Aztlan

An island civilization in the Atlantic Ocean from which the ancestors of the Aztecs arrived in America following a destructive flood. A clear reference to Atlantis, Aztlan was remembered by the Aztecs as "the Field of Reeds," "Land of Cranes" (denoting its island character), and "The White Island." On the other side of the world, the ancient Egyptians referred to an island in the Atlantic Ocean from which the first gods and men arrived at the Nile Delta as Sekhet-aaru, or "The Field of Reeds." To both the Aztecs and the Egyptians, reeds were symbolic of wisdom, because they were used as writing utensils. Atlantis was likewise known as "The White Island" to North African Berbers, ancient Britons, and Hindus of the Indian subcontinent."

At present Mayans are belonged to Central America, and they were great experts in building pyramids and preparing calendars for about several thousand years. There were many similarities found between Egypt and Atlantis (under the sea) and other cultures. One could find a plethora of books on this subject. What I intend to bring forward is to draw similarities between Atlantis and Mayan culture. The cosmology was initiated in the land of Atlantis, and the surrounding lesser kingdoms learned these false doctrines from them. In 2012, around the world, many nations were afraid of the end of the World because of the Mayan calendars and its wrong beliefs. Atlantis was the mother of all these wrong beliefs. As the Central American region was navigable from the land of Atlantis before its demise, i.e., before 1405 BC. This was shown on the cover page clearly how the North and South American continents were near to Atlantis "before" its deluge and in the next picture "after" the deluge. The bottom line is "if the Joshua's Long occurred in 1405 BC then the Atlantis Deluge was in 1405 BC."

Mayans always have the idea of Atlantis from their ancestors who know about an island, and it was called as a white island and the Field of Reeds. They believed that

Atlantis was destroyed by a flood. Mayan ancestors did not experience the torch of fire because they traveled along the North and South American tectonic plates and observing the only tsunami at that time. But the North African, Libyan and even Egyptians recorded the terrible devastation by fire. This was primarily because the flames came out at the junctions of North and Eurasian tectonic plates and that torch traveled towards the east of Atlantis as the convection lava currents inside the earth gave that direction to these flames. Both fire and tsunami were the main reasons of this Atlantis deluge.

Do not wonder now, how these two civilizations can be compared at present they were at a distance, and there was no scope to have links between them. This fact will be explained gradually in the course of this book.

America's First Civilization: Older Than Believed Possible by Zechariah Sitchin, page 17 (Discovering the Mysteries of Ancient America - Lost History and Legends Unearthed and Explored)

"If an astronaut were to corroborate any aspect of my writings, I would have expected it to be regarding the inter-planetary matters discussed and supported in my other published works. Surprisingly, such a corroboration concerns, of all things, the Olmec of Ancient Mexico. It is tucked away in a recently-released book, *A Leap of Faith*, by Mercury 7s' Crew Officer, Gardon Cooper. My book, the *Lost Realms,* mentions colossal stone head with unmistakably black African features, discovered in Veracruz preceding the Mayas and Aztecs.

They were arbitrarily named by archeologists, 'Olmec.' The academically embarrassing enigma of who they were, how they had come across the ocean, and why, was compounded by the timing of their sophisticated culture-bearers in the New World. If the Olmec people represented the earliest of 'Mother Civilization' of Mesoamerica, the day of their arrival was at first determined to be about 250 BC. However, the most recent carbon-14 testing places Olmec beginnings were at 1500 BC. I have argued for a date twice that old."

The author of this book strongly agrees with the Olmec people beginnings at 1500 BC in Central America. The continent of Atlantis was at a navigable distance up to 1405 BC. But some survivors, incidentally away from the mainland of Atlantis, escaped this deluge and were not aware of the fact that they were traveling along tectonic plates to their present positions. When the two tectonic plates drifted towards the west, and they escaped the terrible fire that burst open at the junctions of North, South American Tectonic plates with African and Eurasian Plates. The land of Atlantis deluged completely, and the fire torched up to Libya and burned many places in North African region. History and investigations reveal these facts to us. This date of 1500 BC well fit my claim of Atlantis' demise in 1405 BC. I do not agree with the Plato's date of 9500 before his time for Atlantis deluge.

Minoan Civilization

Quote: (*The Great Minoan Eruption of Thera Volcano and the Ensuing Tsunami in the Greek Archipelago* - by John Antonopolus, 1991 Klower Academy Publisher, Netherlands)

"The eastern Mediterranean has been the cradle of many great civilizations. The history of the area considered of glorious civilizations. But, sometimes, natural hazards became the cause for new classifications of the political, as well as of the military status quo in the region. The enormous eruption of the submarine volcano on the Greek island of Thera (Santorini) during the Bronze Age, around 1500 BC, is such a natural hazard. The tsunami generated by the eruption literally wiped out the peace-loving Minoan civilization that inhabited the island, Crete. After the sea had subsided, the configuration of the area was altered, and the decline of the Minoan principality on the Archipelago began. The present paper introduces evidence concerning the tsunami and states some of the after-effects which were partly responsible for the decline of the Minoan empire. All the information is gathered from historical sources and recent research works. An effort has been made to include many of the theories introduced by various researchers through time concerning the event. Finally, information has been included from all known research, as well as from the authors' won conclusions, to make the paper useful to future researchers."

Here, we should note that Minoan civilization collapsed suddenly by natural hazards around 1500 BC. There was a link between these volcano eruptions and disappearance of Atlantis in one day and one night. Please be diligent and read the book to arrive a comfortable conclusion.

(Quote: website – Cherubini_et_ al_ANTIQUITY_2014.pdf)

Bronze Age Catastrophe and Modern Controversy: Dating the Santorini Eruption

"The date of the volcanic eruption of Santorini that caused extensive damage to Minoan Crete has been controversial since the 1980s. Some have placed the event in the late seventeenth century BC. Others have made the case for a younger date of around 1500 BC. A recent contribution to that controversy has been the dating of an olive tree branch preserved within the volcanic ash fall on Santorini. In this debate feature, Paolo Cherubini and colleagues argue that the olive tree dating (which supports the older Chronology) is unreliable on some grounds. There follows a response from these authors dating, and commenting from other specialists, with a closing reply from Cherubini and his team."

The Minoan eruption raised many questions because of its intensity in and around the Mediterranean Sea. Many writers and geologists claim that its ash went to ice land also, recent drillings in ice land the volcanic ash found dated back to 1500 BC. Many geologists have ascribed this ash to Minoan eruption near Crete. But this was not comfortable enough to be believed. Here one thing we have to observe that ice land is north of present Azores (land of Atlantis), and it is very clear that that volcanic ash belongs to the Atlantic volcanic eruption and not the Santorini eruption near Crete. However, the date of the eruption of Santorini matches with the deluge of Atlantis in 1405 BC.

(Quote: The Minoan Eruption of Santorini around 1613 BC and its Consequences by Walter L. Friedrich) Website; Friedrich_ satz.pdf)

When did the eruption happen? Over the past forty years, there had been prolonged discussions about when the eruption occurred, and major discrepancies have arisen in the results of scientists and archeologists. While some archeologists used evidence from pottery and the styles of design elements to date the eruption to around 1500–1520, a series of radiocarbon dates, ice-core dating and dendrochronological observations pointed to ages of about 100–150 years earlier.

When we observe the phase underlined above, we can arrive at the exact date of Santorini eruption which is 1405 BC – the date of Joshua's Long Day and the demise of Atlantis. As the Thera island was situated at the junction of African and Eurasian tectonic plates, while North & South American tectonic plates start moving towards west, these tectonic plates in the Mediterranean Sea disturbed, the junction opened giving way to the volcanic ash with devastating speed filling that region with volcanic ash. This eruption was different to the present day volcanic eruptions. So there was a link between Santorini eruption and Atlantis Deluge. There may be two phases of the eruption of Santorini until the junction settles down in the inner part of the earth.

Who was Plato?

"Plato was a prominent philosopher and thinker of the ancient Greek. He was respected as the first person to have given an account of Atlantis. Hundreds of books came out about Atlantis because of Plato's dialogues of Timaeus and Critias. The prominent writer Frank Joseph put some information about Plato in his book *Atlantis- The Encyclopedia.*"

"Together with Socrates and Aristotle, he was the most important philosopher in the Western World. Alexander Whitehead, a prominent twentieth-century metaphysician, declared, 'the safest general characterization of the European philosophical tradition is that it consists of a series of footnotes to Plato.' It is impossible to imagine a more credible source for Atlantis-as-fact. Born in Athens around 428 BC, he inherited the story from Solon, the influential Greek legislator, who heard it narrated during a visit to the Nile Delta, early in the fifth century BC. However, many historians believe Plato traveled to Sais himself, perhaps specifically, to verify the Egyptian account. The existence of this temple record was documented by two other highly influential thinkers. The last major Greek philosopher, Proclus, wrote 800 years after Plato, but in his *Platonis Theologiam* (Platonic Theology), he cited the veracity of Atlantis by pointing out that Egyptian columns inscribed with the story, which was visited and identically translated more than half a century after Plato's death. They were examined by yet another influential thinker, Krantor of Soluntum, described by Proclus as *amicus Plato,* sed magis *amicus* veritas: 'Plato's friend and a powerful friend of truth.' He went to Sais as part of his research for Plato's first biography, near the end of the fourth century BC, and reported that Krantor found the Atlantis story preserved exactly as described in the Dialogues. There may be no other account supported by men of such stellar credentials. Yet, modern skeptics, particularly archeologists, dismiss Atlantis as entirely legendary. They fail to consider that beyond his position as the seminal philosopher of Western Civilization, Plato based his whole body of thought on ruthless pursuit of the truth. Timaeus and Kritias cannot comprise a fictional allegory for his notion of the ideal state, as some critics insist, because the Atlantis he portrays is far from his utopian conception, as developed in *The Republic.* It seems likely, however, that Plato, had he completed the Dialogue, would have used the rise and fall of Atlantis as a historical example illustrating the fatal consequences of civil degeneracy. In the Kritias, he did not inexplicably change from philosopher to historian, and his intended use of the lost civilization to provide a factual basis for his political ideas appears probable. Some of Plato's critics accuse him of inventing the Atlantis story out of whole cloth. Yet Greeks knew about the lost civilization before he described it. At the annual Panathenea Festival in Athens, women participants wore a *peplum*, a broad skirt embroidered with scenes depicting Athena's victory over the forces of Atlantis—not a particularly remarkable fact in itself, except that the Panathenea was celebrated 125 years before Plato was born. He was about two years old when 'a major earthquake caused widespread destruction and tsunami inundation around the Gulf of Evvia' (Childress, 19). A nearby island partially submerged and separated from the mainland by the same geologic upheavals was renamed Atlanti, together with its equally devastated gulf, after Atlantis, whose fate it suggested.

Plato appears to have been supported in his account of Atlantis by most scholars of the ancient world, if not all, including the noted historiographer, Theopompus, and the more famous naturalist, Pliny, the Elder. His Atlantis Dialogues were seconded by the renowned Greek writers Diodorus Siculus, Plutarch, and Poseidonus of Rhodes, of whom the Roman historian, Strabo, wrote, 'he did well in citing the opinion of Plato that the tradition concerning the island of Atlantis was something more than fiction.' Only Aristotle, Plato's adversary, was more ambiguous: 'He that created Atlantis also destroyed it.' Critics have interpreted this statement to mean that Plato invented the tale. But the ambiguous 'he' mentioned by Aristotle might just as well have referred to Poseidon, the sea-god attributed in Timaeus and Kritias with the creation and destruction of Atlantis. In 1956, Albert Rivand, Professor of Classical History at the Sorbonne, declared that both dialogues embodied ancient, historic traditions and contained results of the latest contemporary research carried out in Plato's day. As Ivan Lissner wrote, 'That a distinguished French scholar who had spent decades studying the Platonic texts should reach this conclusion is most significant, because it invests the geographical and ontological allusions in the two books with greater weight.' R. Catesby Taliaferro writes in the foreword to the authoritative Thomas Taylor translation of Timaeus and Kritias:

It appears to me to be at least as well attested as any other narration in any ancient historian. Indeed, he (Plato) who proclaims that 'truth is the source of every good both to gods and men,' and the whole of whose works consists in detecting error and exploring certainty can never be supposed to have willfully deceived mankind by publishing an extravagant romance as a matter of fact, with all the precision of historical narrative."

Is Atlantis a Myth or Reality?

It is a matter of ongoing debate whether Atlantis is myth or reality. The earliest mention of Atlantis is attributed to Plato, written in around 360 BC. The author is going to prove by this book, Atlantis is a real and cent percent real place, and we have to find out the exact location of the Atlantis in the present Atlantic Ocean. This book helps us to achieve that task. Please be patient and go on reading this book to unveil the mystery.

Most theories propose the place of existence of Atlantis in Mediterranean, but the author supports the idea of its place in the Atlantic Ocean. Many geologists and experts identified a sunken island west of the Straits of Gibraltar as a potential place for the location of Atlantis. A common view of the cause of the Atlantic destruction was by a great earthquake and Tsunami. The author is thrilling to introduce the reasons why the earthquakes and Tsunami occurred on one day and night making the disappearance of Atlantis a possibility.

Many believe that Athens and Atlantis were parallel civilizations; there were classes of people, including artisans, farmers, warriors and royal people. These two civilizations learned how to mine silver and gold. It is believed that they had horse-drawn chariots; they built bridges, aqueducts, canals and roads and had ships to navigate international trade and voyage at that time.

Some sources tell us the people of Atlantis were directly descended from Poseidon, the Greek God of sea. In case we depend on Plato's time, the story of Atlantis was a myth, because 12,000 BC there were no domesticated horses and chariots. There were no roads, certainly no canals and bridges. In fact, according to all archeological findings till 12,000 BC, every single person on the earth was a hunter and lived by hunting. Biblically, these vast time periods were not acceptable since the creation of earth was reckoning for 4000 BC.

So it seems Plato's date was wrong. Please wait for the exact time the author mentions for the destruction of Atlantis and it is going to fit all the archeological outputs. One view that has been kicked around for a long time and supports the date author is going to propose for the destruction of Atlantis. The author believes that there was a correlation between the destruction of Minoan culture on Crete whose cataclysmic end occurred in volcanic eruptions in 1500 BC. Certainly, there was a good relation between the disappearance of Atlantis and the volcanic eruptions in Minoan land.

The destruction was evident, but the time of Plato is wrong because the social conditions described for Atlantis and Athens by Plato cannot be any earlier than 1600 BC. So if we can solve the problem of the year of destruction and the causes of the sudden deluge, then we can prove that Atlantis was not a myth reinstating our faith in a 100% real land and real culture.

Our concern is to establish that Atlantis was not a fable but a fact, a historical fact. When the author perused through different books and available materials, it was found to be a magnificent culture that flourished until greediness and arrogance entered into this people and culture.

The Author of Atlantis- The Mystery Unravelled, Jurgen Spanuth, page 22

Quote: Confident in the trustworthiness of Plato's beliefs, numerous scholars, have attempted to solve the riddle of Atlantis. According to Ceram, about twenty thousand books have been written since Plato's days on the subject; Braghine and Paul Herrman put the figure as high as twenty-five thousand using all possible means at the disposal of mankind, attempts were made to tear the veil from the secret. Societies were founded, conferences held, and research expeditions equipped to further the task. According to newspaper reports, in 1950 alone, three large expeditions were trying to find Atlantis. Egerton Sykes believed the sunken isle to be in the neighborhood of the Azores, more than I0,000 feet deep and tried in vain to find traces of it, using radar equipment and depth charges. A descendant of Tolstoy is reported to have set off from the Bermudas because an American airman was said to have sighted walls and temple ruins in the South Atlantic during the last war. The Frenchman Henri Lhote equipped an expedition to the Sahara, where, in the waterless stone desert of Tanzerouft, he hoped to find the sunken island of Atlantis. The American scholar and politician Donelly called on the navies of the world, "instead of waging wars, to achieve useful cultural work by searching for the relics of Atlantis on the bed of the ocean."

Ancient Northeast Americans Preserved Flood Story

This American ancient myth states that the earth began to rock to and fro like a ship in the sea. And also the fires dwindled out of the earth was mentioned in this story. This was a perfect fit for our assumption of tectonic plate opening at the tri-junction where Atlantis continent was situated. The Atlantean land disappeared under the waters in a single day and night.

Frank Joseph mentioned this story in his book, *The Atlantis* - Encyclopedia as follows:

Algonquian Flood Myth

"Native tribes of the American Northeast preserved a tribal memory of their ancestral origins on a large island in the Atlantic Ocean. After many generations, signs and portents warned the inhabitants of impending disaster. Some magnitude of the evacuation that took place is suggested in the 138 boats said to have been prepared for the emergency. According to Algonquian elder Sam D. Gill, it began when "the Earth rocked to and fro, as a ship at sea." The quakes became so powerful the island "was cut loose from its fastenings, and fires of the Earth came forth in flames and clouds and loud roarings." As the flotilla of refugees made good their escape, "the land sank beneath the waters to rise no more." The survivors eventually landed along the eastern seaboard of North America and married among the indigenous peoples to become the forefathers of the Algonquian tribes. There is no more succinct and credible version of the Atlantis catastrophe and its aftermath."

The ancient records or oral traditions of Mesoamerican people reveal to us the reality of flood and earthquakes in the Atlantic Ocean. They believed that the people who drowned became fishes and other living organisms in the oceans. But that was not the case. The Aztec people also mentioned the same words that Plato used, "One single day and night the Atlantis disappeared." If their ancestors were not passed on this story orally and by symbols, this was not possible to stand alive this story. The Central American region was close to Atlantic continent and at a navigable distance at that time. Some people escaped the deluge and traveled far off distances along with the tectonic plates. They did not know that they were traveling on moving continents. But they observed that continents (earth) were moving, and earthquakes shook the North and South American continents with lesser magnitudes.

Frank Joseph define this story of earliest Mesoamerican beginnings as follows in his book *The Atlantis - Encyclopedia.*

Annals of Cuauhtitlan

"An Aztec chronicle of earliest Mesoamerican beginnings, from when the first civilizers arrived on the eastern shores of Mexico after a destructive flood. "For fifty-two years the waters lasted," it reports. "Thus, they [ancestral people] perished. They were swallowed by the waters, and their souls became fish. The heavens collapsed upon them, and in a single day they perished. All the mountains perished [under the sea]." These "Annals" are compared to the Babylonian Deluge story of Ishtar (the Sumerian Inanna); wherein the goddess laments how her people were "changed into fish" by a great flood that overwhelmed a former kingdom. So too, the Aztecs chose virtually the same words Plato used to describe the destruction of Atlantis "in a single day and night." That "the heavens collapsed upon them" also suggests a celestial event as part of the Deluge."

Where was Atlantis Situated?

Greek philosopher Plato wrote about Atlantis in 360 BC describing it as an island situated in front of the straits called the Pillars of Hercules.

Pillars of Hercules (from *Atlantis Encyclopedia* by Frank Joseph)

"In Plato's *Dialogues*, we learn that Atlantis was located "beyond the Pillars of Heracles," known today as the Strait of Gibraltar. The "pillars" were twin columns of enormous dimensions flanking a massive caldron of perpetual flame that not only burned in homage to the demigod Heracles, but marked the western limits of the Classical World. This monumental sacred site stood on a high cliff and could be seen for many miles out at sea by sailors aboard approaching ships, and, therefore, served as a kind of lighthouse beacon. Its exact location is unknown, but it must have been built in either coastal Spain, near Tarifa; or in Morocco, around

Cetua or perhaps even Tangier. Heracles' far western shrine may have survived until the collapse of the Classical World when it was finally destroyed by either earthquake or invading Visigothic barbarians in the fifth century AD – carrying forward an ambiguity in its construction ownership. Because the Strait of Gibraltar was known to Phoenician sailors as the "Pillars of Melkharth," their version of the Roman Hercules, some writers believe it was set up by the Carthaginians, who were known to have venerated a pillar cult. But so did their predecessors, the Atlanteans, according to Plato. The structure may have originally been built by them, but was subsequently renamed by the Greeks and Romans after the defeat of Carthage, in 146 BC."

These pillars were known as the Straits of Gibraltar in bygone times. Using Plato's detailed account of Atlantis as a map, searches have focused on the Mediterranean and Atlantic as the best possible sites for the city. Plato said the island he called Atlantis "in a single day and night disappeared into the depths of the sea." Many geologists and writers claimed the Atlantis at different spots worldwide.

But the fact remains unchanged – that Atlantis disappeared in one day and one night. That's why this incident was linked with Joshua's Long Day, because of the tectonic plate movement the Atlantis Island was drowned in the Atlantic Ocean, and it was moved further west.

Some say it's in the Caribbean, some say at the South Pole while others say it never existed at all. But an astonishing recent discovery of the coast of Cuba just might solve the mystery of the great sunken civilization. One of the more likely places would be around the Azores Islands. The Azores are a group of islands belonging to Portugal located about 900 miles west of the Portuguese coast. Some people believe the islands are the mountain tops of the sunken continent of Atlantis. The author is also assuming this site as the place of Atlantis. However, there should be some search and evidence before confirming this site. Volcanic eruptions were the main stumbling block to dive into this sunken world. Thousands of tons of mud would have accumulated in this sunken island constructions, and it was a challenge to the scientists and geologists to remove the mud. Let us look forward to the latest technology which helps us to go down to the mud to see the sunken paradise of Atlantis.

To find out the exact place of the Atlantis in the Ocean the geologists have to study the movement of North American and South American tectonic plates and their direction of movement. Before Joshua's Long Day South and North American continents were closer to African and European continents. With Joshua's supplication, God moved the above said two tectonic plates for about a day in a westward direction and reached present positions.

Conspiracy About the Time of Existence of Atlantis

As go to the details of the Atlantis from the different sources we came to know that Athenians were 1000 years older than Egyptians. But Egyptians had retained their ancient knowledge more faithfully than the Greeks. The story of Atlantis tells us the facts occurred in the Earth's ancient past. At some time in the common heritage of both cultures, Earth had experienced a fiery catastrophe from heaven. In this story, the priest explained that the disaster caused by not only fire but also by water as well.

In the Biblical global flood, there was no mention of fire. There mentioned the gates of heaven and the springs of the earth. The entire world was deluged by water. But here we have to think about the timing of the Atlantis deluge and the way it was disappeared. So the Plato mentioning of 9000 years may be the lunar cycles of the Egyptian reckoning at that time. Some scholars did not agree with the time of Atlantis mentioned by Plato. Why was Atlantis destroyed? Was it the arrogance of power mentioned by Solon that brought about their destruction! This may be the divine judgment because of their false doctrines and beliefs they practiced in those days. They predicted the end of the age by their wrong doctrines and belief system. The Mayan people learned the same beliefs from them and practiced them and prepared a calendar so that the world would be destroyed in 2012. The mainland Atlantis giants ruled the outer ring areas with proud and greediness. The central kingdom ruled by giants always treated the outer kingdoms with pride and arrogance.

There was a conspiracy that prevailed till now about the time of deluge of Atlantis. Some scholars support the lunar cycles mentioned by Solon, and they reckon about 900 years instead of 9000 years. If we think about this, there were no written records of the incident and it was not possible to survive the story of Atlantis by the oral tradition of the people for about 9000 years! I strongly agree with the other researchers that the time of deluge of Atlantis should be around 1400 BC–1500 BC. Moreover, 9000 years before means Plato indicates the Stone Age people not possible for them to build such type of gigantic constructions mentioned in the story. It is read that they prepared dockyards to travel through to the inner lands of the Atlantis.

They did not believe in the promise of God that there would not be any deluge to earth by flood. There they developed the ships to navigate to other lands for war purposes, and also they wish to escape any deluge come over them as in the days of Noah. They thought that deluge came by water and it would rain for forty days and forty nights. Why Almighty God took such long time to deluge earth because He wanted to survive the seed of the man through Noah's ark. In the case of Atlantis, it was done one terrible day and night. Now let us discuss the location of Atlantis and the reasons for the sudden demise of it.

Let us take the help of some other authors and writers to our claim of Atlantis deluge in 1405 BC. In a write up by Nicholas Tschoegl, he commented as follows:

"The idea of a rich and powerful island civilization that perished in a sudden cataclysm has held man's imagination ever since 'Atlantis' was first mentioned in the writings of Plato. Accumulated scientific and archeological evidence now indicates that the 'Lost Continent' may have been located on the islands of Crete and Thera, which were devastated by volcanic eruption in about 1450 BC. Recent archeological discoveries on Thera, including surprisingly beautiful frescoes, add to the compelling evidence of a peaceful ancient civilization which corresponds in many striking respects to Plato's description of Atlantis. Although the number of books that have been written about Atlantis could fill a small library, they are all based on a single literary source: The Platonic Dialogues, *Timaeus,* and *Critias.* Plato (427–347 BC) was related through his mother's family to Solon, the Athenian poet and socioeconomic reformer who became chief magistrate of Athens in 594 BC Solon had learned the story of Atlantis from a priest of Neith (the equivalent of the Greeks' Athena) while visiting Egypt, and it was passed down in the family of Plato. The *Timaeus* and *Critias* contain the essence of the Atlantis legend. If the destruction of Atlantis is, accordingly, taken to have occurred 900 and not 9000 years before Solon, the date of the catastrophe becomes 1500 BC. It is difficult to be exact about when the Thera eruption took place, but that it was about 1450 BC is currently accepted."

Atlantis was Bronze Age Civilization

As mentioned above, there were many speculations about the time of existence of Atlantis. Many writers supported the view of Bronze Age. Some were thought to a civilized society in the very ancient past who knew how to fly and very technological developed society. When we observe the conditions mentioned by Plato of its culture and other aspects, it only belonged to the Bronze Age civilization not more than that. The author strongly agrees with all other writers who support the Atlantis belonged to Bronze Age civilization.

Frank Joseph in his book *Atlantis – The Encyclopedia* defined Bronze Age as follows:

The Bronze Age

"Bronze was the Ancient World equivalent of plutonium in the Atomic Age. Before its appearance, tools and weapons were made of either stone (usually granite and flint) or copper. Bronze was entirely superior to both, and whoever possessed it, wielded a quantum advantage in military and industrial affairs. But it was difficult to manufacture because it depended on the quality of the copper used and was combined with zinc and tin. None of the three minerals occurred in abundance throughout Europe and the Near East, where demands from every kingdom for the new metal erupted after its discovery at the turn of the fourth millennium BC. The only real sources of tin were found in southern Spain and parts of England. As some indication of the copper's importance, the modern island of Cypress derives its name from 'Kippur,' the Assyrian word for copper because it was one of the few locations where it was mined in some abundance. But even there, its quality was not consistently first-rate. Despite insufficient supplies of copper, zinc and tin, by 1500 BC, the great powers, and even most of the lesser ones, had outfitted their often massive armed forces with vast arsenals of superb bronze weapons. The superpowers - Egypt, the Hittite Empire, Troy, Minoan Crete, Mycenaean Greece and Assyria - ranged against themselves millions of bronze swords, spears, and battering rams, their soldiers outfitted with bronze helmets and shields. In ostentatious displays of wealth, kings would sometimes bedeck the walls of their cities with great sheets of gleaming bronze, or fill their squares and temples with the bronze statues of gods and heroes. An enormous industry arose, specializing in the manufacture of bronze tools essential to craftsmen, artisans and armorers from Ireland to. Mesopotamia. Clearly, native mineral deposits, especially of copper, were insufficient, both in quantity and quality, to have even begun to keep pace with such a grand-scale supply and demand. For more than a century, historians have asked themselves, 'Where did the ancients obtain the copper necessary to make so many bronze items?' The Old World Bronze Age began around 3000 BC, reached peak production from the 16th–13th centuries BC, then came to an abrupt end about 1200 BC. It was not logically superseded by the advent of the Iron Age, but followed instead by the precise opposite of all human progress: a four-century-long Dark Age, during which the lamp of civilization was extinguished in Europe, Asia Minor, and the Near East, excepting only Pharaonic Egypt, which had nevertheless entered a decline from which she would never recover. Moreover, iron had been known to Egyptian workers since early dynastic times, while Hittite arms were already bolstered by iron lance-heads and axes. Curiously, the Bronze Age exactly parallels another, although intimately related mystery: the excavation of prodigious amounts of the world's highest grade copper ore from the Upper Great Lakes Region of North America. Beginning circa 3000 BC, people, described in Menomonie Indian oral tradition as fair-complexioned 'Marine Men,' applied sophisticated mining techniques that would not be seen again until the Industrial Age. They extracted a minimum of 500 million pounds of copper, all of which vanished with the white skinned miners by 1200 BC when the pits were suddenly abandoned. That is the same date for the final destruction of Atlantis, whose inhabitants Plato described as world's wealthiest mineralogists. Clearly, it was the seafaring 'Marine Men' of Atlantis who discovered the Upper Peninsula's rich mineral deposits, mined them, and sold high-grade copper to the tool and weapons manufacturers of Europe, Asia Minor, and the Near East. Together with copper, tin was mined along Michigan shores, evidence for the manufacture of bronze, with which the Native American Indian residents were unfamiliar. The North American source was jealously preserved as a state secret upon which the Atlantean monopoly depended on. When Atlantis was destroyed around 1200 BC, the secret went with her, and the Bronze Age ended for lack of quality copper supplies.

The three most influential and interrelated aspects of ancient times - the Bronze Age, Atlantis, and the Upper Great Lakes copper mining - share the same time parameters."

The above definition of Bronze Age clearly declares the Atlantis belonging to the Bronze Age. They mined bronze and copper to prepare swords and spears marketing them to neighboring countries. Many geologists have excavated these remains from the surrounding kingdoms. They even prepared Bronze sheets to export for covering temples and other religious activities which were the common practices in those days. Bronze vessels can also be found in parallel civilizations of that day. Atlantis people were called as fair-skinned people and also called as Marine people as they knew about mining techniques. They grew to become the affluent ones by exporting bronze items to Mediterranean countries. Many countries have their trade routes to Atlantis for these amazing items. In the above article, Frank Joseph is also supporting the idea of the deluge of Atlantis in 1200 BC. The author would like to modify this statement. When Joshua's Long day occurred , so did the Atlantis Deluge in the Atlantic Ocean. We have to go for unknown history of Atlantis by the known history of Joshua's Long Day. The historians can fix a year and date for the Joshua's Long Day. Then it will become relatively easier for us to determine the date of Atlantis Deluge in the Atlantic Ocean. So the readers can understand the story of Atlantis belonged to Bronze Age people.

Even Bible records the incident that Moses lifted the Bronze serpent to give life to the deceased by the bite of the serpents. Use of bronze is recorded in this period and around the Mediterranean countries. So the author of this book proposed a date of Atlantis deluge in the Bronze Age, which was linked with Joshua's Long Day.

Chapter 3

Location of Atlantis

There were many speculations about the location of Atlantis. Many suggested many places around the world. But the author intended and determined to locate Atlantis in the Atlantic Ocean as this book clarifies about the location with clarity. This assumption is going to match with many scientific expeditions made in this era of the scientific age. The author appreciates every explorer of Atlantis because of their zeal that revealed the secret behind the story. First of all, Plato's story is fact and not fiction. Atlantis was real, and some ruins under the sea and some ruins mixed with lava which came out of the junctions of American, Eurasian and African tectonic plates support this fact a degree more.

The Beauty of the Atlantis!

Atlantis is said to be the only place that can stand as a comparison to earth's beauty. Fruits and vegetables grew in abundance in its mineral-rich soil; fragrant flowers and herbs on its mounts bloomed, and the landscape was wooded with beautiful trees; wild animals and lush forests were adorned with rivers and lakes; underground streams of mineral-rich water irrigated the soil. Miraculously, there were hot and cold streams and baths for all the inhabitants – even horses. The soil of Atlantis was rich in precious metals, and the Atlanteans were wealthier with gold, silver, brass, tin, and ivory than any people that reigned before or after. Their principal royal palace was an architectural marvel of size and beauty. Besides being skilled metallurgists, the Atlanteans were accomplished engineers. A huge and complex system of canals and bridges linked their cities and capitals to the sea and the surrounding countryside. There were magnificent docks and harbors for voyages that carried on a flourishing trade with overseas countries.

In the course of time, the people of Atlantis began to lose the love of wisdom and virtue that they had inherited from Poseidon. As their divine nature was human, nature got an upper hand, they became greedy, corrupt and dominating. The Atlanteans were no longer satisfied with ruling their great land of plenty. They set about waging wars over other prospering continents on the other side of the Ocean. Then their armies struck eastward into the Mediterranean region, conquering North Africa as far as Egypt.

(Graphic:- Page no: 126 Rings of ancient Atlantis

Hot and Cold Fountains in the Land:

The history of Atlantis tells us they had fountains of cold and hot water. They knew the ways of using these thermal fountains for the pleasure of kings and the people. They constructed buildings and planted many trees. This land was fertile land because it was formed by volcanic activity in the beginning. But how can one say this? If we can observe the tectonic plate junctions, these junctions pass through the land of Atlantis. In the beginning or during the global flood or after the global flood the land of Atlantis was formed by Volcanic activity. There were king's baths and separate baths for women, apart from multiple temples dedicated to numerous deities.

The Atlanteans grew to the level of a superpower in that region, and they tried to subdue many nations in addition to their colonies in the vicinity at that time. They had a robust army and giant workers who could take up big projects of constructions such as temples and pyramids in the continent. With abundant mineral and food supply, plantations were a rich site of fruit trees, green pastures for the cattle and streams of cold and hot water. Interestingly, this land was comfortable for all seasons. But the hot springs were possible only at the place of volcanic activity and at the junctions of Tectonic plates. It is one of the main evidence of the location of the junction of the above mentioned tectonic plates. Here in India, at the Himalayas, there were many thermal glaciers. This was because these ranges were situated at the junction of two tectonic plates namely Indian Plate and Eurasian Plate. So this is evident that the thermal springs on Atlantis were possible because there was volcanic activity in the past unknown and the thermal springs due to tectonic plate junctions. So we can conclude that the real place of Atlantis was at the tri-junction of North, Eurasian and African tectonic plates.

They prepared some concentric rings in the land through which the ships easily reached the interior land. The Kings, who were treated as Gods, lived in the central part of the kingdom to rule over the land and people. Many people served the Atlantean kings as slaves, and thus, slavery prevailed in that kingdom.

The harbors of the land had plenty of goods to do business with the visitors and store war equipment in the dockyards.

Atlantis (from *The Atlantis- Encyclopedia* by Frank Joseph)

Literally 'Daughter of Atlas,' the chief city of the island of Atlas, and capital of the Atlantean Empire. From the welter of accumulating evidence, a reasonable picture of the lost civilization is beginning to emerge: As Pangea, the original supercontinent was breaking apart about 200 million years ago, a continental mass trailing dry-land territories to what is now Portugal and Morocco was left mid-ocean, between the American and Eur-African continents pulled in opposite directions. This action was caused by seafloor spreading, a process that moves the continents apart by the operation of convection currents in the mantle of our planet. The resultant tear in the ocean bottom is the Mid-Atlantic Ridge, a seismic zone of volcanic and magmatic activity extending like a narrow scar from the Arctic Circle

To the Antarctic. The geologic violence of the Ridge combined with rising sea levels to eventually reduce the Atlantic island's dry-land area. Time frames are very controversial among Atlantologists, and this issue is addressed in the text, that follows. Conservative investigators tend to regard

Atlantean civilization as having come into its sometime after 4000 BC. By the end of that millennium, the Atlanteans were mining copper in the Upper Peninsula of North America; establishing a sacred calendar in Middle America; building megalithic structures such as New Grange in Ireland, Stonehenge in Britain, and Hal Tarxian at Malta; as well as founding the first dynasties in Egypt and Mesopotamia's earliest city-states.

The island of Atlas was named after its chief mountain, a dormant volcano. The chief city and imperial capital were Atlantis, arranged in alternating rings of land and water interconnected by canals. High walls decorated with gleaming sheets of polished copper alloys and precious stones, featuring regularly spaced watchtowers, encircled the outer perimeter, which was separated from Mt. Atlas on the north by a broad, fair plain. The inner rings were occupied by a spacious racetrack, for popular events of all kinds; military headquarters and training fields; bureaucracy; the aristocracy; and the royal family, who resided in a palace near the Temple of Poseidon, at the very center of the city. This temple was the most sacred site in Atlantis - the place where holy tradition claimed that the sea-god Poseidon mated with a mortal woman, Kleito, one of the native inhabitants, to produce five sets of male twins. These sons became the first Atlantean kings, from whom the various colonies of the Empire derived their names. The first of these was Atlas, earliest ruler of the island in the new order established by Poseidon. From this passages, we come to know the beauty of the ancient Atlantis and the culture prevailed at that place. We can understand more clearly about the continent of Atlantis through the following graphic:

(Graphic:- Page no: 124 Ancient Map Showing Atlantis Against Pillars of Hercules)

Present day the Azores was the remnant of Atlantis, which can still be found at the junction of three tectonic plates. There was a great conspiracy about the time of existence of Atlantis among many writers. The people of Atlantis knew well about the copper and bronze mining, and they used bronze weapons to prepare dockyards and canals in this land. It is believed that even iron weapons developed around this time and were used by them. They were great warriors on the land and sea, subjugated all other lands around them. And more importantly, they encouraged the king worship, and they worshiped Sun God through their magnificent temples.

Why they constructed dockyards with much strain and time, because they were sea people and they traveled through seas in those days. Moreover, they were afraid of another deluge which occurred in Noah's days. They thought that these dockyards could help them to escape from any flood of the measure of Noah's days. They forgot about the God's promise of not sending deluge again and the rainbow of the God.

The outer area of Atlantis was densely crowded with habitations, and they were ready for war and voyage in the sea at all times. At the time of Atlantis' existence, the other lands (present Central American area) and continents were at a navigable distance.

We can observe from the graphic that the land of Atlantis is navigable from Europe and Africa. And also, it was the navigable distance to Central and North American continents before the deluge of the Atlantis. Many hundreds of years later we were locating ancient temples and pyramids on the land of Central and North America. How this miracle happened is explained in the forthcoming chapters.

Indian *Puranas* Mentioned the Atlantis

To have traced the mention of Atlantis in the Hindu literary traditions of the *Puranas* is a matter of pure joy for the author. The Atlanteans were called as Aditya's in Indian's *Puranas*. Atlantis was mentioned as Tripura in Indian writings. Even though the tectonic plate knowledge was not available in those days they unknowingly wrote the Atlantis was situated on the tri-junction of three tectonic plates namely North & South American tectonic plates and Eurasian and African Tectonic plate junctions. What coincidence! Or it might have been assumed that this land was formed as three concentric circles as which the historian generally depicted as the Atlantis.

Frank Joseph mentioned these things in his book called *The Atlantis Encyclopedia.*

Aditayas

Also known as the Daityas, offspring of Vishnu, the water-giants' somewhat equivalent to the Titans of Greek myth (like Atlas and the other kings of Atlantis), the Aditayas are mentioned in *Vishnu Purana* and *Mahabharata*, two of the oldest and Most revered ancient Indian literary traditions. The latter work describes them as the inhabitants of Tripura, the Triple City in the Western Ocean, doubtless the Atlantic island of Poseidon (of the trident). The Aditayas were destroyed after they engaged in a war that culminated in the sinking of Tripura, the same story retold by Plato in his account of Atlantis.

Atala

"The White Island" described in the great Indian epic *Mahabharata* and in the epic poems, the *Puranas*, as the mountainous homeland of a powerful and highly civilized race located in "The Western Sea" on the other side of the world from India. *Vishnu Purana* located Atala "on the seventh zone" of heat, which corresponds to 24–28 degrees' latitude, on a line with the Canary Islands. *Mahabharata* likewise locates Atala, "an island of great splendor," in the North Atlantic, where its inhabitants worshiped Narayana. This was the "Son of the Waters" and "the blessed supporter" (Atlas, "the supporter"), who was later responsible for a world-flood. Atala itself sank in a violent storm. All this unquestionably bespeaks Atlantis and its destruction. In Hindu myth, Atala was the center of seven realms. "They are embellished with the magnificent palaces in which dwell great snake-gods [compare with Valum, 'Kingdom of Serpents,' from which Votan, the Quiche Mayas' founding father, arrived in Middle America]—and where the sons of Danu are happy. There are beautiful groves and streams and lakes." This description mirrors Plato's description of Atlantis in Kritias. The six regions surrounding Atala correspond to another Atlantean allegory.

Chapter 4

Egyptian Link with Atlantis

During 1800–1700 BC, a new king came into power in Egypt. The Bible says he didn't know Joseph in Exodus 1:8

"Now a new king arose over Egypt, who did not know Joseph." This verse was a peculiar and surprising to Bible commentators and us. Because Joseph was a prime minister of Egypt in his lifetime and he survived Egypt and other surrounding countries by preserving food stock during terrible famine hit the middle east region. He built Godowns in Egypt to provide food for the people of Egypt. Joseph was a noble and well-noted person who learned the future and saved many thousands from starving.

"Then Pharaoh said to Joseph, I am Pharaoh; and without your order, no man may do anything in all the land of Egypt." (Genesis 41:44)

But this sentence is saying that the new king did not know Joseph. He must be outside of the Egypt and came to power by conquering and ruled the people in quite a different way.

Above mentioned period quite fitted to the parallel dynasties in Minoan and Atlantis. The history told us that the Atlantis lost their virtue and became greedy and not satisfied with their wealth in their island.

The Bible commentators also commented on Exodus 1:8

Notes on Barnes, The Bible:

"The expressions in this verse are special and emphatic. 'A new king,' is a phrase not found elsewhere. It is understood by most commentators to imply that he did not succeed his predecessor in the natural order of descent and inheritance. He 'arose up over Egypt,' occupying the land, as it would seem, on different terms from the king whose place he took, either by usurpation or conquest. The fact that he knew not Joseph implies a complete separation from the traditions of lower Egypt..."

Pulpit Commentary:

Verse 8: There arose a new king. It is asked, 'Does this mean merely another king, or a completely different king, one of a new dynasty or a new family, not bounded by precedent, but free to adopt and likely to adopt quite new principles of government?' The latter seems the more probable supposition; but it is probable only, not certain. Assuming it to be what is meant, we have to ask, what changes of dynasty fall within the probable period of the Israelite sojourn in Egypt, and to which of them is to most likely that allusion is here made? Some writers (as Kalisch) have supposed the Hyksos dynasty to be meant, and the "new king" to be set, or Salatis, the first of the Hyksos rulers. But the date of Salatis appears to us too early. If Joseph was, as we suppose, the minister of Apophis the last Hyksos king, two changes of dynasty only could come into consideration- that which took place about 1700 BC (or according to some historians 1600 BC).

This new king has different principles, and he was very cunning and not having any mercy even towards children. The King of Egypt ordered midwives and Egyptian citizens to throw the Israelite male babies into the Nile River. It was a cruel act before God. For the stability of their country, he wanted to kill the innocent babies mercilessly.

Here one thing the author would like to stress is, at that time, only Atlantis had the power to conquer other lands at that time. As history tells us, the armies of Atlantis traveled eastward into the Mediterranean region, conquering North Africa as far as Egypt and southern Europe up to the Greek borders.

Over the centuries, scholars have attempted to locate the real Atlantis believing the account was based on a real ancient superpower.

In fact, the story of Atlantis was reported by Plato in the fourth century BC, who said he read it in the writings of Solon, who proclaimed to have received the story from the Egyptians. At that time, Egypt was reachable by North African Mediterranean shore by the people of Atlantis. After the disappearance of the island of Atlantis, few survivors reached Egypt and brought the story of Atlantis to Egypt. By oral tradition, this story reached Plato. As a philosopher of that day he converted the story into two dialogue works namely *Timaeus* and *Critias* in 360 BC.

One thing we have to remember that in case the destruction of Atlantis was before 12000 BC, there was no possibility of passing this story to the fourth century BC. So there should be the earlier date of Atlantis existence and its deluge. That was going to be declared through this book.

This new Egyptian King did a crime in the sight of God, and the man reaped what was sown in due seasons. Lord Jesus said in Mathew 18: 6 "but whoever causes one of the little ones who believe in Me to stumble, it would be better for him to have a heavy millstone hung around his neck, and to be drowned in the depth of the sea."

The author believes that Lord Jesus mentioned the land of Atlantis and its destruction due to the arrogance its ruler who killed male baby children of Israelites in Egypt. The heavy millstone is nothing but the Atlantis. As history tells us this land was erected in the sea with three concentric rings of canals, it therefore, seems like a millstone.

Without fear of God, this new King in Egypt assassinated small and innocent children by throwing them into the Nile river for the safety of his kingdom by believing wrong concepts about Israelites. We can easily understand that each Israelite parent wept for their male kids, and they groaned for their lost children. It was very hard and heartbreaking time to bear the consequences of losing loved ones as the hearts of the Israelites were becoming stubborn. They failed to follow the commandments of God in the wilderness. This king badly affected the minds of thousands by showing his cruelty towards foreign people and fellow human beings in the land of Goshen.

We know how God miraculously raised Moses and brought the children of Israel from the bondage. The author would like to explain how God punished people of Atlantis by destroying them in one day and night in the next chapter. Please continue to read, you will know the mystery how the land of Atlantis disappeared in one day and night.

Moses Encountered a New King in Egypt

Israelites lived nearly 300 years in Egypt and their status changed in this land under the new king. Their old privileges were now gone, and what remained of them were lower than slaves in the reign of this new king. This new dynasty has long forgotten Egypt's debt to Joseph and his services to Egypt.

Things rapidly changed in Egypt. The new king behaved rudely towards ready-made economic labor force residents in the area - the Israelites. The existence of such a large alien group in the land has for some time made the new king uneasy. Here, his cruel planning organised them into gangs, under group leadership to dig out mud and to make the bricks for his construction projects. No matter how hard they worked the population explosion took place, then this King tackled the problem in more direct ways (Ex 1:15-22). So now all Hebrew male babies were cast into the Nile. That is Pharaoh's decree towards the Israelites. But Moses' life saved by his mother's faithful and resourceful act, i.e.,, preparing a water-tight basket to save Moses.

Moses was forty when he attempted to strike his first blow for freedom (Ex 2: 10-12). He failed and further forty years passed before standing before the king.

New King's Pride

Moses went to Egypt from Midian to liberate his people by Almighty God's command. Pharaoh heard and rejected Moses request. He showed the sort of man he was: "Who is the Lord...? I do not know Lord, and I will not let Israel go." (Ex 5:2)

It was a serious crime to question the existence of Almighty God. So God began a series of judgments to teach Pharaoh and his people whose Lord is, and to show them the extent of his power of overall creation. Nine times God acted, Pharaoh and his magicians and all the Gods of Egypt were powerless to reverse his judgments. God warned the king to obey His command by sending ten plagues into the land of Egypt. The plagues probably occurred over a period of about a year. In each case, God chose to use natural disorders to confound the king and the Gods of Egypt. He caused the Nile-God to bring ruin, not prosperity: the frogs to being diseased instead of fruitfulness and the power of Re, the Sun god, was blotted out. The whole sequence of events occurred and followed a logical pattern which could have started with unusually high flooding of the Nile. God was demonstrating his absolute control. He distinguished between His people and the Egyptians. Several times in these chapters God is said to have hardened Pharaoh's heart and made him stubborn. When God ordered someone to obey, he has to obey by submitting his will. But King acted against the command of God. Due to his stubbornness, the punishment spread its doom over the nation, and finally, they lost their firstborn in the land of Egypt. The Egyptian wanted to send off the Israelites by giving their ornaments because they feared God.

But the pride of Pharaoh made him pursuit after he is leaving Israelites and he tried to cross the red sea with his army. As God drove back to the waters, He ensured that they crossed safely, and the wall of waters fell rushing upon Pharaoh's forces, Israel learned the truth of Moses' words: "The Lord will fight for you; there is no need for you to do anything." (Ex 14:14)

The Egyptian history tells us the following facts:

Second Intermediate Period (1786–1567 BC)

"The 13th dynasty marked the beginning of another unsettled period in Egyptian history, during which a rapid succession of kings failed to consolidate power. As a consequence, during the Second Intermediate period, Egypt was divided into several spheres of influence. The official royal court and seat of government were relocated to Thebes, while a rival dynasty (fourteenth), centered on the city of Xois in the Nile Delta, and seems to have existed at the same time as the thirteenth.

Around 1650 BC, a line of foreign rulers known as the Hyksos took advantage of Egypt's instability to take control. The Hyksos rulers of the fifteenth dynasty adopted and continued many of the existing Egyptian traditions in government as well as culture. They ruled concurrently with the line of native Theban rulers of the seventeenth dynasty, who retained control over most of the southern Egypt despite having to pay taxes to the Hyksos. The conflict eventually flared between the two groups, and the Thebans launched a war against the Hyksos around 1570 BC, driving them out of Egypt. This date may be the earliest and the nearest to 1400 BC but would need investigation. Driving out the king Hyksos should be in between 1500 BC to 1400 BC. Then the Atlanteans tried to win the land of Athens but the Athenians fought against these sea people, and they safeguarded their kingdom. After this incident, Plato reported that this land suddenly disappeared from the human history. The remains of Atlantis were under the sea mixed with lava and volcanic mud. Excavation of this site remains impossible, and the glory of Atlantis will remain buried under the waters of Atlantic Ocean."

Here, observe the phrase "driving them out of Egypt." Why did the Egyptian people drive this new king away? The author's claim is he may be the Atlantean king who came over to Egypt and annexed the power in Egypt. In case, our assumption is true the wandering of Israelites in the wilderness for about 38 years ultimately leads to a date of Joshua's Long Day on 1405 BC.

Let us see the reasons why the people drove him out.

- Because of his pride, Egyptian land was devastated due to ten plagues from God
- Egypt lost its glory and prosperity
- The firstborn of the land died at Passover and every family immersed in sorrow, and they came against the new king

The Egyptian army drowned in the Red Sea due to king's order of pursuing the Israelites

All these reasons made the Egyptians revolt against this new king and drove out of Egypt. The author proposed that this king returned to the island of Atlantis and continued his rule in some part of the island without any change in his mind and with continuing unrest.

The punishment upon this race was not over because they committed a serious crime by throwing innocent male babies into the Nile and this king challenged the command of Almighty God. Thus, God was going to punish this nation in a terrible way which will be explained in the next chapter.

The above claim has to be examined by the experts in geology and by the historians. This is a claim by the author because of similarities between these two regions and period. So this claim gives open debate to agree or disagree whether the new king (Ex 1:8) is from the land of Atlantis or any other king who conquered the land of Egypt.

Plato's Critios says he learned the story of Atlantis from his grandfather, who had heard it from the Athenian statesman Solon (300 years before Plato's time), who had learned it from an Egyptian priest.

Peruvian and Central American Link with Atlantis

(website: www.africaspeaks.com – by Steve Lautenschlager)

When comparing the written languages of Egypt and South/Central America, even more, similarities were discovered. In both cultures, hieroglyphics were used. The Egyptians used hieroglyphics on temples, pillars, and statues. Similarly, Mayas used hieroglyphics in tombs, on monuments, medallions, buildings, and on pottery. Both cultures also used their written languages for practical purposes. In Egypt, business records and letters have been found, (Egyptian Language and Literature, 1979). Similar to this is also the exact day on which the year started; Hawk. The Egyptian and in many South and Central American tombs, hieroglyphics indicate the name of the deceased and the date of death (Adams, 1986es, 1963).

Rituals and practices play an important part in any culture. Among the ancient cultures of Egypt and South/ Central America, there were many rituals and practices that were alike, such as circumcision, astrology and having annual agricultural fairs (Donnely, 1949). A more significant similarity that is common to both cultural areas is the astronomical and directional orientation of edifices. In Maya culture, knowledge of the heavens developed long before AD 250. This knowledge was used in planning and construction of complex pyramid structures (Hammond, 1986). In the Teotihuacan culture of Mexico, buildings are grouped along a north-south axis (Toth& Nielen, 1985), and in Egypt the Great Pyramids at Cheops are just four minutes west of perfect northerly alignment and have other directional and mathematical relationships to the moon, the planets, and the stars (Toth & Nielson, 1985).

Burial in underground tombs is a practice common to Egypt, Peru, and Mexico. The rituals of burial in these cultures were also much the same. All three embalmed and mummified they're dead. They also went to great extremes to seal tombs so that what was within would be preserved (Adams, 1986; Donnely, 1949).

The third major facet of similarity as a technology similarity was the construction of pyramids. Among the pyramids, one can also find striking similarities. On both sides of the Atlantic Ocean, there are step pyramids constructed of several mastaba-like structures. In both cultures, many of these step pyramids stand around 200 feet tall, and evidence indicates that they underwent several changes of the plan throughout their construction (Toth & Nielsen, 1985).

The use of stones for building the pyramids is also common in both cultures. The stones themselves and the construction techniques used, not only in pyramids but other structures as well exhibit very similar technology. The Egyptians and the Tiahuanaco culture of Peru were capable of building with stones weighing from 2–100 tons. The precise placement of these stones is equally impressive. The Tiahuanacans fit their stones so precisely that a razor blade could not be slipped between them. In Egypt, the stones are so accurately joined that there is never more than 1/50 of an inch between blocks (Toth & Nielsen, 1985).

When comparing the technological heights scaled by both cultures, it is apparent that neither culture surpassed the other in knowledge. The Egyptians, however, exhibited the technology on a greater scale than the smaller civilizations of South and Central America.

Though very few of the similarities have been noted, it can be seen that explanation is warranted and that their might have been some connection between Egyptian and South/Central American cultures. Perhaps that connection was Atlantis, a place of common origin. Archeologists and historians consider the Americas to be the Mayan place of origin; however, mystics theorise that the Mayas originated from Atlantis (Toth & Nielsen, 1985). Ignatius Donnely, who lists 626 references in his book comparing the culture's similarities (1949), supports a theory which states that "both the ancient Egyptian and American India cultures originated in Atlantis, and spread east and west when Atlantis was destroyed" (Cayce, Edgar Evans, 1969, p.18).

Before pursuing the theory further, it is necessary that one has a detailed understanding of Atlantis. This is because there are relationships between the two cultural areas and Atlantis, which refer to legends of Atlantis location, time of existence, and destruction."

From the above long quote, we can understand that there was a relation between Egypt, Peru and Central American region. Already we have discussed the link between Egypt and Atlantis. We have learned that there was an indelible relation between Peruvian and Atlantis and Central America with Atlantis. As I have mentioned earlier, the Central American region was closer to the land of Atlantis before its deluge in 1405 BC (if it was the correct date of Joshua's

Long Day). The Mayans learned cosmological knowledge from the Atlantis civilization. Above mentioned cultural similarities are because of the influence of the Atlantis upon the surrounding lower kingdoms which were subdued and ruled by Atlanteans. Ancestors of Mayan people were the live witnesses of the Atlantis Deluge. This can be deduced with clarity in the following lines. While these two tectonic plates namely, North and South American plates traveled westward and these people survived in this land, and they continued their culture which they learned from their mother civilization, Atlantis.

The next day they saw the rubbish and carcasses of man and cattle at the shores of Central America. They portrayed a picture on the stone to show the deluge of Atlantis to the future generations. Mayans knew well about the Atlantis and the details that were lost as there was no scope to record all these things. They were the lower tribe to Atlanteans and they learned cosmology and belief system from the land of Atlantis. So the Mayans continued the customs of Atlanteans as they might have participated in the rituals of Atlanteans.

Chapter 5

God's Timing to Establish Israelites – Chosen People

Do not get amazed to find the author's mention of the establishment of State of Israelites on the face of the earth in this book. From the beginning, God is fighting against the Nephilim, who were the offsprings of Sons of God (angels) and daughters of Adam. This race and their activities were very rude, and their thoughts were evil continually.

Already mentioned in the previous chapters, these Nephilim existed after the flood also. These off springs of fallen angels taught men how to make war and how to prepare weapons to kill one another more effectively and took human wives to pollute mankind's bloodline so that Messiah won't come to this earth. In other words, fallen angels wanted to destroy God's plan of salvation. They eventually attempted to destroy all earthly life on this world.

(Quote: Language of God in- History- Chapter 4- Watchers, page 246)

"In an almost successful attempt to thwart the arrival of the Messiah and only begotten Son of God, the fallen watchers took human wives and had unlawful sex with them, which resulted in the birth of the first race of Giants. The Greeks called this first race of Giants, the Titans. However, the fallen angels were not satisfied with this level of perversion and wanted to increase the genetic corruption going on in the world. They, therefore, began to splice mankind's genes together with those of beings that were very cunning and violent. These genetically mixed species- which God did not design - acted contrary to natural laws. This is why they eventually had the desire to kill and destroy all that yah had created.

The monstrous, bloodthirsty Giants that resulted from the sexual promiscuity of the fallen angels with women as well as their genetic experiments were called by many names in the Bible, including 'Nephilim,' 'Anakim' or simply 'Giants.' Keep in mind, however, that in the Bible only the pre-flood giants are called Nephilim. Those born after the flood were called Anakim because they descended from Nephilim males and human females, meaning that they were related to the watchers. As a result, the Anakim were smaller, less powerful and less long-lived than their Nephilim for bearers."

According to the above quote, we can come to a conclusion that God did not tolerate the unlawful activities of Nephilim, and He wants to fulfill His plan of salvation at the right time and right place. We can observe the phrase that after the flood there were Nephilim on the earth. That's why Genesis 6:4 wrote:

...The Nephilim were on the earth in those days, and also afterward...

These Anakim were there in the land of Canaan. So God led the Israelites from the land of Egypt with wonders and miracles. The second Generation from Egypt under the leadership of Joshua they conquered the land of these Anakim.

"And there we saw the Nephilim (sons of Anak, who come from the Nephilim), and we seemed to ourselves like grasshoppers, and so we seemed to them" (Num 33:13 ESV)

Ten kings and their kingdoms of Atlantis, Plato narrated, should be the descendants of Nephilim as the scripture tells us the Nephilim existed after the flood. The descendants of Nephilim in Atlantis and the Anakim in the land of Canaan have to be terminated at the time of sending the Messiah to this world is nearing in God's time table. The reader may be thrilled to find a correlation between the Atlanteans and the Anakim in the land of Canaan. We should remember the time mentioned by Plato (9500 before his time), which was pre-historic, if one carefully examines the people of Atlantis. They learned to quarry tunnels in hard rocks, and they made concentric rings so that the ships may go inside the interior lands of Atlantis. These projects were not possible without bronze age weapons in their hands. The people of Atlantis might be strong and big in size but without weapons, it was not possible for them. This continent was initially formed by the volcanic activity being it was at the junctions of three tectonic plates namely North, South and Eurasian plates already mentioned in this book.

Solon's Time of Atlantis Demise – Its Probability

When we observe the catastrophe incidents occurred in the Mediterranean Sea, we may speculate about the timing of Atlantis. Already we learned that this culture flourished during the Bronze Age. Many think that Atlantis on the island of Thera and its time fit to the Solon's time of 9000 lunar cycles of Egyptian reckoning. But Thera was a small island in the Aegean Sea, and it won't fit the story of Plato existed beyond the pillars of Hercules. The Egyptian priests might have made a mistake in their interpretation into the Greek language as they translated the Egyptian sign for 'hundreds' of 'thousands.' The Thera eruption had also taken place in between 1400 BC to 1500 BC. But this small island of Santorini was never fit to the story of Plato. But the devastation in Atlantis and Thera occurred in the same time period. There was a link between Atlantis' demise and Mediterranean disturbances in those days. But Atlantis and Santorini were not the same.

The devastation of Thera, Crete and Atlantis might be at the same time. Crete is available for investigations and brought out many theories, but Atlantis was immersed in the deep ocean and many difficulties in exploring it. The author proposes the time of volcanic eruption that affected the island of Thera in about 1500 BC was in fact the doom of Atlantis. Because it is noteworthy that the Thera and Crete at the junction of Tectonic plates of Eurasian and Africa. But this place was not Atlantis. According to Plato's description, Atlantis existed as big land mass and against the pillars of Hercules. Thera explosion was the supporting incident of Atlantis demise by the movements of tectonic plates completely westward and the plate junction opened in the Mediterranean Sea and the eruptions took place around 1400 BC–1500 BC. This period, hence, fits well in the context of the Deluge of Atlantis.

Here, it is important to note that not only eruptions but a tidal wave in the Mediterranean Sea were most likely to have been hit. These tidal waves and storms were caused by the tectonic plate movements in the Atlantic Ocean. The tectonic plate movements can initiate large-scale tsunamis and the author of this book confirm the tsunamis of greater measure which was not occurred in this modern period.

History tells us around 1500 BC, the Minoan culture at its flourishing state on Thera and Crete but the volcanic eruptions led to the doom of the Minoan empire. The tidal waves caused by the explosion and earthquakes and the ash from the volcano eruption were likely to have inflicted severe difficulties upon the people suddenly. Here, sudden happening of this incident also supports the tectonic plate opening in the Mediterranean Sea.

About 3600 years ago (about 1500 BC), a massive volcanic eruption devastated the island of Santorini in the Aegean Sea near Greece, which was at the junction of African and Eurasian tectonic plates. At this time, a sophisticated society of Minoans lived on Santorini. The Minoan civilization vanished suddenly around the same time. So there should be a link between the demise of Atlantis one day and night and the sudden disappearance of Minoan civilization.

Plato mentioned the pride of Atlantis and warned other nations not to try for the subjugation of other nations. Excessive power and wealth directly led to pride. Pride, in turn, resulted in nurturing of political relations of the surrounding countries. So the people of Atlantis arrived to a point that God should take an action to stop their arrogance and wrong belief system.

In conclusion, we can understand that 950 years before the time of Plato means 950 + 430 = 1380 years BC completely fit the events in the Mediterranean Sea. Moreover, already mentioned, 11,000 years BC was not in support a technologically advanced society. That should be Stone Age or ice age at that time. There was no scope of preparing the continent as Plato narrated with Stone Age weapons. Many were assuming that these people knew every advanced technology and even they used to fly in the air. The author did not support such development in those days, but they were entirely rooted in the Bronze Age.

Joshua Faced Anakim

(Quote: got questions.org, who were the Anakim/Anakites)

"The Anakim were a formidable race of giant, warlike people (Deu 2:10, 21; 9:2) who occupied the lands of southern Palestine near Hebron before the arrival of the Israelites (Josh 15:13). The Anakim ancestry has been traced back to Anak, son of Arba (Jos 15:13; 21:11), who at that time was regarded as the 'greatest man among the Anakim." (Josh 14:15).

This name "Anakim" resembled mean "long–necked," i.e., "tall." The Hebrews thought then to be descendants of Nephilim, a powerful race who dominated the pre-flood and post-flood world (Genesis 6:4, Num 33:13). When the twelve Israelite spies returned from exploring the promised land, they gave a frightening report of "people great and tall" whom they identified as the sons of Anak (Deu 9:2). The Israelites were seized with fear and believing themselves to be mere "grasshoppers .... In their sight" (Num 33:13), rebelled against God (Deu 1:26-28) and refused to enter the land God had promised them.

The Israelites were exhorted by Moses (Deu 1:19) not to fear the Anakim, but they refused to trust God's promise (Deu 1:32-33). As a result, God became angry (Deu1: 34-39) and prohibited the "evil generation" from entering the Promised Land, Joshua and Caleb were the only exceptional

(Deu 1: 35-36). Because of their fear of the Anakim and their rebellion against God, the Children of Israel were forced to wander for another 38 years in the wilderness.

"During the conquest of Canaan, Joshua expelled Anakim from the hill country, and Caleb finally drove them out of Hebron completely. However, a small remnant found refuge in the cities of Gaza, Gath, and Ahsod (Josh 11:22). Many Bible scholars thought that the Ankim's descendants were the Philistines giants David encountered (2 Sam 21:15-22), including Goliath of Gath (1 Sam 17:4-7)."

As the author already mentioned God had been fighting against Nephilim from the beginning without mercy because there was a great abomination to spoil the entire human race. This had to be stopped, as all human beings were helpless in fighting against the strong Nephilim. So God performed a miracle and moved the tectonic plates by ordering inner structures of the earth by His word and make the Sun stand still for about a day.

So the time arrived to eradicate the last batch of Giants in Canaan and the Nephilim on the land of Atlantis. God performed this miracle of moving tectonic plates in the Atlantic Ocean to exterminate the Giants in Atlantis and the Anakim in the land of Canaan through the operation of Joshua's Long Day. Many speculate about the time factor, but the author explained clearly about this in the previous chapters giving out many historic evidences and facts. This brings us to scrutinize the link between the Atlantis Deluge and Joshua's Long Day.

Chapter 6

Atlantis Demise @ Joshua's Long Day

There were many assumptions and speculations about the existence and demise of Atlantis. We have to understand that Atlantis was not an Antediluvian world. During the global flood, every human being including Nephilim on the earth destroyed. As the author mentioned earlier, after the global flood the descendants of Noah, after the attempt of building Tower of Babel, they were searching for new lands and continents to live. In the post-flood arena, while going westward from Babel traveling from place to place, after a certain period they found a nice landscape or continent against the pillars of Hercules. At the time of reaching this land, these people found this continent was navigable with small boats and ships from the shores of Europe. They might be traveled through the shores of Mediterranean Sea in those days. Anyhow they reached this beautiful land flourishing with green pastures and different kind of trees as it was a land formed by volcanic activity. This continent was formed due to the lava expelled from the junctions of North America, Africa, and Eurasian tectonic plates.

This continent may be formed during creation period or the global flood. This continent was full of rocky mountains and plenty of plants and glaciers. It must also be observed that this was a land of hot and cold water fountains. So they inhabited the land and cultivating it, farming and cattle breeding were going on.

As Genesis account reveals to us that after the flood they were Nephilim (Genesis 6:4) on the face of the earth, we can understand that after 1500 years of the global flood again Sons of God intermarried the women on this continent and again began a race of Nephilim (Anakim). It is noteworthy that Atlas was a Nephilim.

God never tolerated the hybrid generation of fallen angels who intended to pollute the human race. It is read in the newspapers in the past that scientists tried to live with apes in Africa then the terrible disease HIV came into this world. Whenever the scientists or fallen angels tried to spoil the human race which was created in the image of God, there should be a reaction evident from the heaven. Many people are rejecting Salvation plan of God that is up to them whether accepted to enter heaven or rejected to be perished. But when the earth was in jeopardise because of the acts of some fallen ones there should be an action.

As a part of the divine operation in removing the Nephilim from the earth and a time came to establish Promised Land for Israelites, God took this decision of deluging this land. The pride, greediness and sun worship, animal sacrifices and false theories about future and framing calendars and assuming dates for the end of the world, these activities were viewed seriously as the source of these things were fallen angels. All these activities came to the notice of God Almighty and decided to remove this other Babel from the face of earth.

This occurred at the time of Joshua the God's warrior. Joshua 10: 11-13 reads: "And it came to pass, as they fled from before Israel, and were in the going down to Beth-honor, that the Lord cast down great stones from heaven upon them unto Azekah, and they died... Then spake Joshua to the Lord in the day when the Lord delivered up the Amorites before the children of Israel, and He said in the sight of Israel, Sun, stand thou still upon Gibeon; and thou, Moon, in the valley of Ajalon. And the Sun stood still, and the moon stayed until the people had avenged themselves upon their enemies, Is not this written in the book of Jasher? So the Sun stood still in the midst of heaven, and hasted not to go down about a whole day."

It appears to have been midday or after the Sunrise did not proceed to set for completed day, which many commentators take to be approximately a 24-hour period, rather than just a daylight period. Many cultures have records of legends that seem to be based on this event. For example, there is a Greek myth of Apollo's son, Phaethon, who disrupted the Sun's course for a day. And since Joshua's tenth chapter is historical, cultures around the globe should have long days and nights evidently. We have long days in the African continent and New Zealand Maori people have a myth about how their hero Maui showed the Sun before it rose while the Mexican Annals of Cuauhtition records a night that continued for and extended for an extended time.

It should also be noted that the Amorite were Sun and moon worshippers. For these "gods" to have forced to obey the God of Israel must have been a devastating experience for the Amorites, and this might well have been the reason God performed this particular miracle at Joshua's time. The Israelites were almost at the point of the occupation of the land of Canaan by the help of God.

What Christian Scholars Told About Time of Demise

(Quote: got questions.org, "Does the Bible Mention the Lost City of Atlantis? Is There Any Evidence for Atlantis?")

"The city of Atlantis was a mythological island nation first mentioned in Plato's writings around 360 BC. He claimed to have based his information on manuscript given to the Athenian Solon (638–558 BC) by an Egyptian priest. Atlantis supposedly had conquered Italy and North Africa but was pushed back by Athens shortly after that; the island disappeared into the sea.

Plato speaks of Atlantis in the dialogues *Timaeus and Critias.* In the text, Socrates ponders if a perfect society could ever exist, and Critias tells the story of Atlantis. According to Critias, Atlantis was about 230 miles long 340 miles wide and lay in the Atlantic Ocean, west of the Rock of Gibraltar. According to the mythology, Poseidon's sons, including Atlas, lived there. It was destroyed around 9600 BC by earthquakes and a flood. Plato's contemporaries were split as to whether Plato believed Solon's account. The early Christian Scholars Clement and Tertullian seemed to think Atlantis was real. There is a discussion today as to whether Solon mistranslated the date in the Egyptian hieroglyphics, counting hundreds as thousands; if Solon was in error, then Atlantis' destruction was closer to 1500 BC."

So here from the above quote we can understand the Solons account about Atlantis demise is in error. Anyhow the date proposed by the scholars was very near to the date of Joshua's long day. Ancient historical records were not perfect so we can take them as plus or minus 50 to 100 years. The Atlantis was disappeared from the Atlantic Ocean in a terrible day and single night. This fact links with the Joshua's long day. By god's help, the Sun and Moon stayed in the space for about one day. The Bible was written regarding geocentric experience (earth as a center to the universe)and on observational knowledge because at that time all believe that Earth was the center and all other heavenly bodies moving around it. But at this time of space exploration, we have knowledge about the earth rotation.

(Quote: Atlantis: The Mystery Unravelled, page 30, The desiccation and the Great Fire, Historical Basis of the Atlantis Legend)

"The contemporary documents declare with certainty that such catastrophes did, in fact, occur towards the end of the 1300 BC (i.e., 1390–1410 BC). One source says of the desiccation and the great fire: 'A terrible torch hurled flames from the sky to seek the souls of Libyans and to destroy their tribe.' Edgerton explains that lightening from the sky had affected the Libyans and destroyed their tribe. Similar details may be found elsewhere. "The heat burned like a flame on their land. Their bones burned and melted in their limbs."

"The heat in their land burned like a fire in an oven." And, concerning the North people: 'Their forests and people were destroyed by the fire.' 'Before them spread a sea of flames.' Repeatedly, we find it recorded that the enemies of Egypt were burned or afflicted by the great fire. But Egypt also suffered. An eye–witness, has reported that walls, gates and columns were destroyed by flames, the sky was in chaos, no fruit or food could be found, in a single day everything was destroyed, and the land left to dry out like cut flax."

From the above quote, we can understand that Libya was affected badly and severely. Libya was near to Atlantis, and the fire raged from the tectonic plate junctions pushed out in the direction of Libya and Egypt. Unlike from the Volcano, it was like a torch coming out with tremendous speed and that fire may have even reached western Egypt in those days. The fire travelled like an arrow towards Libya and Egypt.

So we can come to the conclusion that Joshua's Long Day was a historical fact, and we will discuss how the Sun stood still and Moon in the land of Canaan, revolved around the earth as usual. So we assume the date of disappearing of Atlantis one day and night must be on the day of Joshua's Long Day, which occurred in 1405 BC. This matches with the destruction of Minoan and Crete cultures in the Mediterranean Sea. In this context, we must think about the Plato's story of Atlantis demise in one single day and night. This phrase gives much scope to research again about the facts of Atlantis. We know that the volcanic eruptions started slowly, and they lasted for months and even years. Here as far as Atlantis was concerned, it was disappeared in one terrible day and night. This point was the key to this book. Joshua asked the Lord to make the Sun stood still, and the Atlantis was destroyed in one day and night. So there was a link between Joshua's Long Day and the Demise of Atlantis by severe earthquakes and tidal waves.

Let us take the help of other experts in this matter, here I am going to be quoting some scholar's ideas about Joshua's missing day.

Joshua's Missing Day Fact

(Quote: Joshua's Long Day.pdf, Harmony of Science & Scripture, published in 1936)

By Harry Rimmer

"This is a book by Prof. C A Totten of Yale, written in 1890, which establishes the case beyond the shadow of a doubt. The condensed account of his book, briefly summarised, is as follows:

Professor Totten wrote of a fellow professor, an accomplished astronomer, who made the strange discovery that the earth was twenty-four-hour out of schedule! That is to say, there had been twenty- four hours lost out of time. In discussing this point with his fellow- Professor, Professor Totten challenged this man to investigate the question of the inspiration of the Bible. He said, 'you do not believe the Bible to be the word of God, and I do. Now there is a fine opportunity to prove whether or not the Bible is inspired. You begin to read at the very beginning and read as far as need be, and see if the Bible cannot account for your missing time."

The astronomer accepted the challenge and began to read. Some time later, when the two men chanced to meet on the campus. Professor Totten asked his friend if he had proved the question to his satisfaction. His colleague replied, "I believe I have proved that the Bible is not the word of God." In the tenth chapter of Joshua, I found the missing twenty-four hours accounted for. Then I went back and checked up on my figures, and found at the time of Joshua there were only 23 hours and 20 minutes lost. If the Bible made a mistake of forty minutes, it is not the book of God: Professor Totten said, "You are right, in part at least. But does the Bible say that a whole day was lost at the time of Joshua?"

So they looked and saw that the text said, "about the space of a whole day." The word 'about' changed the situation and the thirty-eighth chapter of the prophet Isaiah. In this chapter, Isaiah has left us the thrilling story of King Hezekiah, who was sick unto death. In response to his prayer, God promised to add fifteen more years to his life. To confirm the truth of His promise, God offered a sign He said, "go out in the court and look at the sundial of Ahaz. I will make the shadow on the sundial backup ten degrees! Isaiah recounts that the king looked, and while he looked, the shadow turned backward ten degrees, by which ten degrees it had already gone down! This settles the case, for ten degrees on the sundial is forty minutes on the face of the clock! So the accuracy of the book was established to the satisfaction of this exacting critic.

Notice both include the same three numbers:

- A whole day missing overall
- 23 hours, 20 minutes missing at Joshua's time
- Forty minutes missing at Hezekiah's time

Whether the scientists agree or not the infallibility of the scriptures, the author believes that it is true, and word of God lives forever. There were some stories about a missing day discovery in supercomputers and by NASA. But some are saying that was an 'urban myth' or a hoax. Anyhow I believe the word of God as it is and as it was! Moreover, in Joshua's time the Sun stood still and the moon stayed there was a miracle done by God. Whenever God performed a miracle on the earth, there should be evidence upon the earth and its evidences were real today. Now we are searching for the clear cut evidence in the earthly realm. I am going to explain how the continents moved one day and night against the earth rotation along with the atmospheric layer.

(Graphic:- Page no: 123 Map Showing Joshua's Long Day and Nights Worldwide)

Just observe the solid black circles show locations with tales of a long night; open circles with white color inside plot tales of a long day shows the location of a long sunrise tale. Recently, another long sunrise tale was reported in Hawaii.

Let us discuss how these long days and long nights occurred worldwide in a detailed manner in the following passages:

(Quote: The Day the Sun Stood Still...Joshua's Long Day... Page 35)

In 1940, Harry Rimmer summarised these traditions as follows:

"In the ancient Chinese writings, there is a legend of a long day. The Incas of Peru and the Aztecs of Mexico have a like record (long night), and there is a Babylonian and a Persian legend of a day that was miraculously extended. Another section of China contributes an account of the day that was miraculously prolonged, in the reign of Emperor Yeo.

Herodotus recounts that the priests of Egypt showed him their temple records and that there he read a strange account of a day that was twice the natural length."

Here, we should observe that one side of the earth were long days, and another side of the earth were the long nights. The people at that time did not know that the earth was spherical. This reveals us that how the acts of God are perfect and it was a small thing in the sight of God. How the man is limited, we can understand from this incident. It is clear that man had not been able to understand the miracles of God even after thousands of years later. So we have to understand the Omnipotent power of God and believe Him.

As far as earth's creation is concerned, how wonderful it is to know that God created the earth surface with eight major and some more minor Tectonic plates. This theory helps us to understand the demise of Atlantis and the Joshua's Long Day in the clear cut way. I am giving little information about Tectonic plates in the next chapter. If you are interested to know more about this theory, please navigate the internet to find sites regarding this theory which will help you to understand my book clearly. Thank you!

Chapter 7

North and South American Tectonic Plate Movements

Already, I have mentioned tectonic plate movements and continental drift in my previous title *Paradise Found* which tells us that while removing the Garden of Eden on the face of the earth, the God moved the Arabian plate and African plate slightly and the dead sea formed as it was situated at the junction of both plates during global flood. From the beginning of the creation, God moved these tectonic plates to assemble the land, and He called it Earth (land). So tectonic plate movement is a recent geological theory by which we can explore many truths about planet earth and the scriptures related to them. (Please visit the website and search for my other title: www. amazon.com/ paradise found by Anipe Steven Premajyothi)

Earth was a marvelous and most beautiful planet ever created by God specially prepared for the inhabitation of His loved children, human beings. I believe that in no other star system it may not be there as earth's conditions if it was not prepared and planned by God. No humans prepare this type of planet by their scientific theories and Biological experiments. When we see it from space, we can see it as a green ball clothed with a white robe here and there (clouds). On the surface of the earth, we have many minerals, rivers and oceans and ice glaciers. This is the outward scenario of the earth. But there was more complicated structure inside it. To understand the sudden demise of Atlantis in one day and one night, we must understand these plate tectonics of the earth. First let us learn about the structure of the Earth.

Plate Tectonics

(From Wikipedia, the Free Encyclopedia)

To understand the North and South American Tectonic plate movements to the present positions during Joshua's Long Day or Atlantis Deluge, we should have minimum knowledge of the plate tectonic theory which describes the large-scale motions of Earth's lithosphere.

"The model builds on the concepts of continental drift, developed during the first few decades of the 20th century. The geo-scientific community accepted the theory after the concepts of seafloor spreading were developed in the late 1950s and early 1960s.

The lithosphere is broken up into tectonic plates. On Earth, there are seven or eight major plates (depending on how they are defined) and many minor plates. Where plates meet, their relative motion determines the type of boundary: convergent (Pacific and African plates), divergent (North and South American plates) or transform (East Pacific Rise and the Mid-Atlantic Ridge). Earthquakes, volcanic activity, mountain- building, and oceanic trench formation occur along these plate boundaries. The relative lateral movement of the plates typically varies from zero to 100 mm annually."

But the North and South American plates moved apart with high speed against to the rotational speed of the earth by the conventional currents occurred in the outer parts of the mantle. The theory of viscosity also helped these plates to move with high speed by God's command. This was a miracle performed by God. Recent available theories sufficient to understand this miracle if we have faith like a mustard seed.

"Tectonic plates are composed of oceanic lithosphere and thicker continental lithosphere, each topped by its kind of crust. Along convergent boundaries, subduction carries plates into the mantle; the material lost is roughly balanced by the formation of new (oceanic) crust along divergent margins by seafloor spreading. (Here, we have to understand that the ocean floor between Atlantic ridge and shores of North and South American contents were newly formed ocean floor, i.e., after 1405 BC). In this way, the total surface of the globe remains the same. This prediction of plate tectonics is also referred to as the conveyor belt principle (Here above mentioned ocean floor came out as new and the Pacific plate along with minor plates, i.e., Nazca, Cocos and Juan de Fuca plates converges into earth's mantle as a conveyor belt). Earlier theories (that still have some supporters) proposed gradual shrinking (contraction) or gradual expansion of the globe.

Tectonic plates can move because the Earth's lithosphere has a higher strength and lower density than the underlying asthenosphere. Lateral density variations in the mantle result in convection. Plate movement is thought to be driven by a combination of the motion of the seafloor away from the spreading ridge (due to variations in topography and density of the crust, which result in differences in gravitational forces) and drag downward suction, at the subduction zones. Another explanation lies in the different forces generated by the rotation of the globe and tidal of the Sun and Moon. The relative importance of each of these factors is unclear, and is still subject to debate."

Key Principles of Tectonic Plate Movements (from Wikipedia, The Free Encyclopedia)

"The outer layers of the Earth are divided into lithosphere and asthenosphere. This is based on differences in mechanical properties and the method for the transfer of heat. Mechanically, the lithospheres cooler and more rigid, while the asthenosphere is hotter and flows more easily. Regarding heat transfer, the lithosphere loses heat by conduction, whereas the asthenosphere also transfers heat by convection and has a nearly adiabatic temperature gradient."

Due to heat transfer and convection currents of the lava inside the earth the tectonic plates namely, North and South American Plates start moving towards the west and at the same time the land of Atlantis submerged under waters in a single day and night. At the same time, the African, Arabian plates and Eurasian plates stand still so that the earth dwellers (in certain places) observed that Sun stood still, and the moon stayed there for about 23 hours and 20 minutes by God's command.

Sea Floor Spreading – Subduction of the Plates

We have to understand the sea floor spreading of the oceanic crust before we can understand how the tectonic plates moved apart on the Joshua's Long day. As the author mentioned, the North American and South American tectonic plates were close to the land of Atlantis before Joshua's Long Day. When Joshua ordered the Sun stood still and the moon in Ajalon, the two tectonic plates once started moving towards westward by the way of sea floor spreading in the mid-Atlantic Ocean. At the same time, the Nazca and Cocoos plates subducted into the mantle. As these belonged to oceanic lithosphere which gone into the inner part of the earth and they melted. During this process of subduction into the mantle and the lava came out to form Rocky and Andes mountains at the junction of American plates and Nazca and Cocoos plates of Pacific Ocean. This process started suddenly, and the Tsunami from the Pacific Ocean stopped by this mountain range. The formation of these mountains may continue for some years, and finally, the American Tectonic plates settled in the present positions. Due to the sea floor spreading of the mid-Atlantic, the land of Atlantis deluged on a single day and terrible night in the day when the Sun stood still, and the moon stayed.

We can know more about sea floor spreading from free Wikipedia as follows:

"Seafloor spreading is a process that occurs at mid-ocean ridges, where new oceanic crust is formed through volcanic activity and then gradually moves away from the ridge. Seafloor spreading helps explain continental drift in the theory of plate tectonics. When oceanic plates diverge, tensional stress causes fractures to occur in the lithosphere. Basaltic magma rises the fractures and cools on the ocean floor to form new sea floor. Older rocks will be found farther away from the spreading zone while younger rocks will be found nearer to the spreading zone.

Earlier theories (e.g. by Alfred Wegener and Alexander du Toit) of continental drift were that continents 'ploughed' through the sea. The idea that the seafloor itself moves (and carries the continents with it) as it expands from a central axis was proposed by Harry Hess from Princeton University in the 1960s. The theory is well accepted now, and the phenomenon is known to be caused by convection currents in the plastic, very weak upper mantle, or asthenosphere.

The new oceanic crust is quite hot about old oceanic crust, so the new oceanic basin is shallower than older oceanic basins. If the diameter of the earth remains relatively constant despite the production of new crust, a mechanism must exist by which crust is also destroyed. The destruction of oceanic crust occurs at subduction zones where oceanic crust is forced under either continental crust or oceanic crust. Today, the Atlantic basin is actively spreading at the Mid-Atlantic Ridge. Only a small portion of the oceanic crust produced in the Atlantic is subducted. However, the plates making up the Pacific Ocean are experiencing subduction along many of their boundaries which cause the volcanic activity in what has been termed the Ring of Fire of the Pacific Ocean. The Pacific is also home to one of the world's most active spreading center's (the East Pacific Rise) with spreading rates of up to 13 cm/yr. The Mid-Atlantic Ridge is a 'textbook' slow-spreading center, while the East Pacific Rise is used as an example of fast spreading. The differences in spreading rates affect not only the geometries of the ridges but also the geochemistry of the basalts that are produced.

Since the new oceanic basins are shallower than the old oceanic basins, the total capacity of the world's ocean basins decreases during times of active seafloor spreading. During the opening of the Atlantic Ocean, sea level was so high that a Western Interior Seaway formed across North America from the Gulf of Mexico to the Arctic Ocean."

(Graphic:- Page no: 125 Which shows Subduction and Volcanic activity - seafloor spreading)

When North American Plate pull apart, several things happen along the mid- Atlantic Ocean. Volcanic activity was severe there as the mantle easily moved to the surface and the land of Atlantis, and the big constructions apparently mixed with lava flowed. As Atlantis situated at the junction of tectonic plates, when the new ocean floor formed at the mid-Atlantic ridge, the North, and South continents moved apart in a day and a terrible night during the Joshua's Long Day.

The North American and South American Plates moved apart as divergent tectonic plates. This divergent boundary formed of mountains in this junctions. The ridge at mid-Atlantic was spread with unusual speed by upwelling of magma from the mantle creates new ocean floor. So as the new ocean floor formed in the mid- Atlantic and the Plates moved apart in one single day and night. Ocean floor spreading occurred on a large-scale during Joshua's Long Day by magma is constantly streaming out to the surface, creating new ocean floor in the Atlantic Ocean.

At the same time, the North and South American plates collided with Nazca and Cocoos minor plates in the Pacific Ocean. These two oceanic lithosphere plates subducted into the mantle along western coasts of these two continents, so that the earth circumference was not changed. When these two plates subducted and melted in the mantle, the extra lava comes out to form mountain range along the convergent boundaries. This happened along the western shores of North and South America. So even the North and South American plates moved thousands of kilometers on that terrible day and night there was no change in the circumference of the earth. The volume of the lava inside the earth is constant. Whenever subduction plates took place, volcanic activity prevailed, and the mountain ranges apparently form along the convergent boundaries the

Tectonic plates. The author claims that the Andes and the Rocky Mountains belongs to this category.

Structure of the Earth

(Quote: Henry David Thoreau wrote)

"Earth lithosphere (outer layer) is divided into mobile plates. Plate tectonics describes the distribution and motion of the plates. The theory of plate tectonics grew out of earlier hypotheses and observations collected during explorations of the rocks of the ocean floor.

(Graphic:- Page no: 120 Picture Showing Earth and Different Layers)

There are three major layers (crust, mantle, and core) within the earth that are identified by their different compositions.

The uppermost mantle and crust can be subdivided vertically into two layers with contrasting mechanical (physical) properties. The outer layer, the Lithosphere, is composed of the crust and uppermost mantle and forms a rigid outer shell down to a depth of approximately melted rocks in the upper mantle that acts in a plastic manner on long time scales. The asthenosphere extends from about 100–300 KM depth. The theory of plate tectonics proposes that the Lithosphere is divided into a series of plates that fit together like the pieces of a jigsaw puzzle."

Now we are dealing with the North and South American plate movements in an unusual speed on Joshua's long day, and the Atlantis was deluged in the Atlantic Ocean. To understand these plates movements, we have to refer to The Internet and the geologists provided valuable theories and lessons on this subject. The main objection may be which force caused to move these plates apart with high speed in single day and night. Here the geologists and scientists proposing the convection currents in the mantle make this possible. This will occur according to the command of supernatural power whenever it is needed. As we believe that God is the creator of this universe, He can do what He intended to do for His purposes fulfill. Some may argue that how it was reasonable to drown a society was flourishing in those days. But we should remember that they propagate false belief systems in those days about future. The Mayan calendar was the main evidence, and this belief system came from their mother civilization Atlantis. We have observed the news and how the people terrified about the end of the world on 21 Dec 2012. This was a sample of the Atlantis belief system. God has His reasons to do something on the earth. Nobody can question Him because He never does wrong.

(Graphic:- Page no: 127 Tectonic plate divisions of the earth)

From the above graphic, we can observe that these tectonic plates namely African, Eurasian and North American Plates had junctions at a certain area that point is the actual location of Atlantis continent as described by Plato's against the pillars of Hercules.

The people of Atlantis did not know that they have their beautiful, wonderful continent was poorly situated at the junction of the three tectonic plates. After the global flood may be at the time of Peleg (Genesis 10:25), the earth was first time divided. During that separation may be the Atlantis continent formed as the lava was coming out from the mantle of the earth at these junctions.

Peleg's grandfather was Salah, and it means "send, scatter, make somebody flee" might be that the scattering of the people happened when Salah was born. It was 37 years after the Flood. They had 64 years to go to their ordered territories by God before the continental drift.

As Plato mentioned the continent was navigable from the pillars of Hercules, and the size of the continent taking into consideration the central part of Atlantis should be at the junction of three tectonic plates, i.e.,, present Azores. It is learned that in the central area, the Giants lived and in outer rings the subjugate tribes around them. The geologists calculated the movement of Tectonic plates was only a few centimeters per year. This rate is true for today. But in the beginning, God said that in Genesis account as a part of the third-day creation "and God said, let the waters under the heavens be gathered together into one place, and let the dry land appear." And it was, so God called the dryland Earth, and the waters that were gathered together he called Seas. (Genesis 1: 8-10)

We should observe for this act it took only a part of a day to God to bring together all the Tectonic plates together. So the tectonic plates gathered or diverged at different speeds as the case may be and this might be done by God and God alone no force in this universe can move these gigantic continental, or oceanic plates move with such high speed. We should not compare earth's tectonic plates present speed to other incidents occurred by God in ancient times. From the beginning, the plates might be moved with different speeds as it was possible with God.

(Graphic:- Page no: 128 North & South American Plate Boundaries after the deluge)

It is clear that the North American Plate and South American tectonic plates were at a navigable distance and having their junction beneath the Atlantis continent. Geologists are at a thought of millions of years of time to spread the continents to present positions. But if we can observe carefully that much of time not necessary as I have explained earlier by taking Genesis account as an example.

It was noteworthy that geologists found that North American and South American plates are divergent towards the west and African plates convergent towards the north. So these two plates traveled towards the west with the certain speed with opposite speed to the rotational speed of the earth towards the east. Here, I should mention that African Plates and other plates another side of the earth stand still for 23 hours and 20 minutes and by miracle of God North & South American Plates traveled west causing the terrible demise of Atlantis in one day and night.

The geologists called the junctions of the plates as ridges. The ridges in the Atlantic Ocean are still active and some volcanic eruptions, and big sounds still being heard by the scientists. The Mesoamerican areas and Mexico were at a navigable distance to Atlantis continent before its deluge as shown in above picture. That is the reason many similarities were being observed between Atlantis culture and Mesoamerican culture. The Mayans learned much of the cosmological knowledge from the mainland of Atlantis. As the North and South American, Tectonic plates move away from the land Atlantis so that these two continents reach present locations in 23 hours and 20 minutes. At the same time, the African and other eastern plates stood still for about 23 hours and 20 minutes. So that Joshua and the Israelites observed the miracle of Sun and Moon stood still in the sky until the God's army exterminate the last batch of Anakim from the face of the earth. While moving away from the land of Atlantis the tribe belonged to Central America experienced severe earthquakes and inaundations of the earth for about a day. The Author believe that some of them were survived from these convulsions, and later they developed as Mayan culture in Central America and Peruvian cultures. Moreover, the author believe that an annual ritual may be going on the land of Atlantis to worship Sun in their land at the time of their deluge.

The following discovery reveals the existence of Atlantis or the cities developed by Atlanteans at the time of their period. Jes Alexander and team found:

(Quote: Abstracting Atlantis: Scientists Find Evidence of Mayan Culture Underwater City)

"Jes Alexander said that they have found the remains of an ancient city on the sea floor in the Western Caribbean. It is important to note that we have found is the remaining of an ancient city that was formerly above sea level, and perhaps as much as 4500–8000 years old. This has nothing to do with another site, found almost ten years ago by a Canadian/Russian team working to map the sea floor near the Yucatan Peninsula. Their site is nearly 2 miles below the sea floor. The site we are working with is much shallower- in between 40 and 70 feet of water. We initially found anomalous objects by mapping a grid and searching the sea floor using simple Google Earth Technology."

Since the junctions of North and South American Tectonic plates were near the Atlantis continent and once they started moving westward the divergent plates formed by new lava from the mantle. Present ocean ridges in the Atlantic Ocean and the up to the shores of these two continents might be younger than other ocean beds relatively. There was a wide scope to find out these facts through further investigations and research.

It is important for us to learn more about the structure of the earth and its Lithosphere. It was developed by Henry David Thoreau:

"Lithosphere and Earth's Construction: The theory of plate tectonics proposes that the Lithosphere is divided into eight major plates (North American, South American, etc.) and several smaller plates (e.g.,, Arabian, Scotia, Juan de Fuca, etc.) that fit together like the pieces of jigsaw puzzle. These plates are mobile, moving in constant, slow motion measured at rates of centimeters per year. The movements of plates over millions of years resulted in the opening and closure of oceans and the formation and disassembly of continents. This theory links Barth's internal processes to the distribution of continents and oceans; it is the big picture view of how Earth works.

Plate tectonics theory joined continental drift to sea floor spreading to propose:

- The plate boundaries are mainly represented by oceanic ridges and trenches.
- Interactions at plate boundaries cause volcanic activity and earthquakes.
- The plates are in motion, moving away from ridges and towards trenches.
- Plates descend into the mantle below trenches in subduction zones.

- Plates typically contain both oceanic and continental Lithosphere.
- Oceanic Lithosphere is continually created and destroyed.
- Continental Lithosphere cannot be destroyed, but continents can be subdivided and assembled into supercontinents."

The North American and South American plates are divergent which traveled westward of Atlantis, and it was done in one day and one night. While moving these two plates towards the west, the junction of Eurasian and African Plates disturbed and here and there plate openings occurred and the volcanic eruption initiated at Thera and the Minoan culture vanished during the same period. As the North American and South American plates moved away from the Atlantis and Tsunamis traveled eastward deluging many lands in Mediterranean and coastal lands of Africa and Europe. As the earth was rotating towards the east the flames of lava torched over the land of Libya and North African land mass. This was evident from the history.

As mentioned earlier, these two divergent tectonic plates moved westward and caused this great catastrophe of major convulsions, earthquakes, and tidal waves during the time of Atlantis demise. We have to think about how these plates move. There should be a force behind every movement. So God's power involved in moving these two divergent tectonic plates towards the west and the Atlantis disappeared in one day and night as explained by Plato. The time of the Atlantis demise should between 1380 BC–1410 BC as other civilizations vanished by major volcanic activities occurred in the history of Mediterranean area. In case Joshua's Long Day occurred in 1405 BC , it was the correct date of Atlantis demise! The date of Joshua's Long Day changes by recent investigations then the Atlantis Deluge also changes.

God has always been known to intervene in the activities of man as we learned from the Global flood in about 3000 BC. There also the main problem was with Nephilim, who were the hybrid generation that existed on earth. I have authored a book *Paradise Found* in which I have mentioned about these plate tectonics revealing a hole that has been formed at the actual location of the Garden of Eden, where the Eden probably disappeared. If you are interested, please visit amazon.com and you will find the mystery unfolded in that book.

Website: www.amazon.com/pradise found by Anipe Steven Premajyothi.

At the time of Israelites' occupation of Canaanite habitations and the pride of wrong belief system peaks in the land of Atlantis, God took a severe stance through a miracle by hearing the voice of His servant Joshua. Certainly there was a link between the demise of Atlantis and the Sun stood still in the land of Canaan at the time of Joshua.

Let us discuss the Joshua's missing day story by exploring the available evidence in the next chapter.

Chapter 8

Joshua's Missing Day Story

Many scientists and Bible Scholars explained this story in different ways in their own perceptive. But this is a fact, that God Almighty did it. Everything is possible with God and these miracles have been in line with natural laws and sometimes against the natural laws. The waters divided and stood as walls either side of the way while Israelites are crossing the Red Sea. It was a miracle. Sometimes the natural laws coincide with the miracles some times it was not, and it may take thousands of years to grasp it to man, how that miracle happened. Here in case of Joshua's Long day, it occurred thousands of years ago beyond the comrehension of the human mind. Here, we should think of the Earth and Moon revolving around the Sun as one unit, but as far as earth is concerned the African Plate stood still, not rotated for about 23 hours and 20 minutes and at the same time two tectonic plates traveled westward so that these continents reach present positions in 23 hours and 20 minutes. Eastward rotation stopped and westward rotation (opposite direction) initiated and minimized the catastrophic atmospheric effect worldwide, and the devastation was limited to Northern Africa and Mediterranean region.

(Quote: Joshua's Missing Day Story by Mr. Harold Hill- Joshualongday.pdf- cell)

"Well, they found there is a day missing in space in elapsed time. They scratched their heads and tore their hair.

There was a no answer. Finally, a Christian man on the team said, you know, one time I was in Sunday school and they talked about the sun standing still while they didn't believe him, they didn't have an answer either, so they said, show us. He got a Bible and went to the book of Joshua (Joshua 10:12-14) where they found a pretty ridiculous statement for any one with common sense.

So, Joshua asked the Lord to make the Sun Stand still! That's right- The Sun stood still, and the moon stayed – and hasted not to go down about a day!

The astronauts and scientists said, there is the missing day! They checked the computers going back into the time it was written and found it was close but not close enough. The elapsed time that was missing back in Joshua's day was 23 hours and 20 minutes- not a whole day. They read the Bible, and there it was about (approximately) a day.

These little words in the Bible are important, but they were still in trouble because if you cannot account for 40 minutes, you will still be in trouble 1000 years from now. Forty minutes had to be found it can multiply many times over in orbits...

As the Christian employee thought about it, remembered somewhere in the Bible where it said the sun went backward. The scientists told him he was out of his mind, but they got out the Book and read these words in 2 Kings 20: 9-11, Hezekiah, on his death-bed, was visited by the prophet Isaiah, who told him that he was not going to die. Hezekiah asked for a sign as proof. Isaiah said Do you want the sun to go ahead 10 degrees? Hezekiah said it is nothing for the sun to go ahead ten degrees, but let the shadow ten degrees backward! Ten degrees is exactly forty minutes! Twenty-three hours 20 minutes in Joshua, plus forty minutes in Second Kings make the missing day in the Universe."

Link Between Joshua's Long Day and Atlantis Demise

Previously, we discussed the time of Atlantis' demise. We did not agree to Plato's claim of Atlantis' demise before 9500 years from 360 BC. The Historical and geological events in and around the Mediterranean Sea leaving evidence that not so far of ancient time but near past the Atlantis deluge occurred. Many geologists and historians speculate about the story of Atlantis living in the minds of people by oral tradition are highly impossible for 9000 years. So the comfortable period for the demise of Atlantis is 1380 BC–1410 BC. Many believing that Minoan and Crete civilizations are parallel to the time of Atlantis. The author completely agrees with the above view of Atlantis demise in near past, i.e., in the above mentioned period.

As we have been assuming that the tectonic plates of North and South America moved westward by deluging a big continent of size Asia Minor and Libya together, one often wonders about the ways in which this shift became possible! What happened to earth's rotation? What about the remaining tectonic plates of the earth? What happened to African plate? In Joshua's time, what miracle happened to Israelites?

Let us answer all these questions in the light of the historical facts that took place in those days. Joshua prayed to God for a miracle to revenge against their enemies as he wanted complete victory on that day over Amorites. Joshua needed some more day time to eradicate the

Anakim and Amorites from the land. From Noah's time, God began fighting against the Nephilim. Moving forward, God performed a great miracle (in man's view) to eradicate Nephilim race in Canaan and the arrogant Atlantis people in their land who were injecting a sense of false belief system and Sun worship. God commanded His creation as he spoke with earth in Exodus 32. Bible records that Lord spoke to the earth many times. As shown in the graphics the Mesoamerican area is close to Atlantis (at a navigable distance) and South American Continent was relatively close to the African continent as the geologists found similarities of plants and fossil record in western Africa and eastern shore of the South American continent. There was a wide scope of research around the Atlantic Ocean beds. The speculation on whether they formed in the recent past (about 1500 BC) or before the global flood. The author believes that present ocean ridges in the Atlantic Ocean to the shores of both North and South American continents were formed in recent past (about 1500 BC). The scope of research in this aspect is infinite and one can only scratch the surface for hidden meanings, interpretations and findings.

Moving on to discuss how the Lithosphere oceanic plates moved thousands of kilometers in a single day and night, one must have an idea of continental drift. Continental drift is a process of continents moving apart yearly at a rate of ten to fifteen centimeters. But during a miracle of Joshua's Long Day, the plate movement was against the rotation of the earth and quite opposite to the speed of rotation of the earth.

As far as African plate and other eastern plates are concerned, they remained static, and the South and North

American Plates started moving suddenly with terrible volcanic eruptions on the continent of Atlantis. As it was situated in the tri-junction of Eurasian, African and North American tectonic plates, the land of Atlantis moved significantly, and the lava came out of the land deluging everything under the sea. The buildings were mixed with lava and some of them reversed in its positions. So we cannot find anything about Atlantis as it once was! It is almost like finding a buttered piece on a hot pizza. This lava torched as far as Libya. That was the magnitude! At the same time, the African plate stood still and helped the Israelites to take revenge over their enemies. The North American and South American plates reached to the present positions in 23 hours and 20 minutes. These two plates overlapped on Nazca plate, Juan de Fuca plate and Cocoos plate in the western shores of North and South America. The atmosphere and along with earth was traveling eastward, and the North, and South American plates traveling westward with the speed so that it can minimize the catastrophe on the face of the earth. Let us understand the Earth's rotation.

How Earth Rotates?

Earth's rotation is the rotation of the planet around its own axis. The earth rotates from the west towards east. The Earth rotates once in about twenty-four hours on the sun and once every 23 hours 56 minutes and 4 seconds.

The ground feels firm and solid beneath our feet. Of course, the earth is rotating, turning once on its axis every day. Fortunately, gravity keeps us firmly attached to the planet, and because of momentum, we don't feel the movement- the same way we don't feel the speed of a car going down the highway. But how fast does the Earth rotate?

We might be surprised to know that a spot on the surface of the earth is moving at 1675 Km/h or 465 meters/second. That's 1040 miles/hour. Just think, for every second, we are moving almost half a kilometer through space, and we don't even feel it. The Earth's circumference at the equator is 40075 kilometer. And the length of time the Earth takes to complete one full turn on its axis is 23.93 hours.

Here these calculations are correct. God performed a miracle to honor prayer of His servant Joshua for a noble cause of removing the last batch of Nephilim from Atlantis and the people of Anakim from the land of a Canaan. It was also God's timing to rearrange final geology of earth to live the inhabitants in safe and security. When we speak of the distances of the continents, the North, South and African, Eurasian Plates were relatively close at that time. So the Mesoamerican Mayan culture had a link with Atlantis, and they did not know that they traveled thousands of kilometers in one single day and a single night. They learned one thing that another side of the World perished and were lost in the waters. Some of them hardly survived and again they predicted about the end of the world in 2012, according to their calendars. The entire world knew that those predictions were wrong, and man cannot decide a date to the end of the creation. It was the job to be done by the creator!

Because of these plate movements, terrible Tsunamis unleashed in the Atlantic Ocean and even reached the islands of Mediterranean Sea. At the same time, the Eurasian and African plate junctions disturbed and earthquakes occurred, and volcanic activity initiated throughout the Mediterranean Sea and parallel devastation occurred in

Crete at the same time. The volcanic ash was found even on the ice land in the layers in the time past. This may be the effect of volcanic activity at the spot of Atlantis, i.e., at the present place of Azores. The ruins of Atlantis were mixed with lava and volcanic ash. So it was difficult to find out and dig out the glory of Atlantis as it was before 1400 BC. The temples and buildings of the Atlantis mingled with lava came out from the junction of tectonic plate movements. Plato gave a keynote that it was destroyed in one single day and a single night. This one sentence made me research about this last continent. Plato's words about Atlantis were true, and they were not fiction. But the timing of its demise was incorrect because it was not possible to survive this story for about 9500 years. The first king of the Atlantis was described as a man standing nakedly, bearing spherical ball on his shoulders. They thought that Atlantean kings were bearing the entire universe. They proclaimed as the Gods of the universe. So these thoughts were very dangerous and lead to man worship on earth.

Some geologists suggested that the North pole slightly tilted in the time past. It may occur during the time of Joshua's long day. Due to this tilting of the North Pole by God's command, the movement of North and South American Plates towards west might occur in one terrible day and night.

"To illustrate the large-scale relationship contains a section through the Earth along a great Circle between South America and Africa. The unevenness of the Earth's surface and the great deeps of the Atlantic Ocean one small enough to be contained within a circular line describing the Earth's surface. For comparison, the figure also contains the iron core of Wiechert and the main atmospheres: the nitrogen sphere, water sphere and an upwardly unconstrained sphere, the theoretical Geokoronium. The zone of clouds (troposphere, is not thick enough to be shown)."

It is very difficult to show the fourth-dimension of Earth on paper. Please refer to the internet if you find difficult to understand certain aspects of the book.

At the time of Joshua, the North and South American plates moved westward with speed so that these continents reached their present positions in a period of about twenty-four hours. The Sun seems to be stood still because the African plate and other portion of the earth stood still by God's command through man of God in Israel. When two American plates moved westward, the Atlantis at the junction of North America, Eurasian and African plates disturbed violently then earthquakes, volcano eruptions in greater measure as the lava came out as gigantic torches which then traveled hundreds of miles and brought destruction to the lands and the people. There might have been an instance of fire rain on North African lands, and many tribes washed away.

Some historians reported that devastation was in no way compared to the destruction of Atlantis to other catastrophes of the earth history. If African plate stopped its movement what happened to the atmosphere which was moving along with earth at that moment? I suggest that the wind and atmosphere probably traveled towards the East and the American plates started traveling westward the violent tsunamis began in the Atlantic Ocean affecting the shores of Africa and the Mediterranean Sea up to the island of Crete. At the same time, Thera eruption took place and great devastation came to this region. Finally, in this region due to the opposite movement of the tectonic plates to the atmosphere the devastation minimized. The American plates experienced earthquakes and inundations without fire. So some of the tribes most probably the Mayan and other tribes living in Central America may survive. With the knowledge, they gained through the land of Atlantis, they constructed some pyramids on both continents in the near past. That is why we observe similarities between the civilizations of the Mayan, Peruvian and Egyptian cultures. Atlantis was the mother of all these civilizations!

How did The Continents Move in That Little Time?

This activity or phenomena was possible only by subduction and moving of the lithosphere as follows:

(Graphic:- Page no: 129 Hemisphere with Convection Currents of Lava in the Mantle)

The continental or oceanic plates are very thin when we compare it with the size of the Lithosphere or the tremendous lava currents flowing inside the earth. As shown in the above graphic under the African and Eurasian plates the fluid lava flowed in a ring as "convection current." So it not difficult to move these thin layers of the oceanic or continent plates towards west. While moving these plates, the tri-junction under Atlantis was wide open, and the continent broke into pieces. Consequently, the civilization along with its people, temples and every structure went slipping under the ocean in one day and night as the Joshua commanded "the Sun stood still and moon."

Here we should observe that revolution of Earth along with the moon around the Sun was not ceased, but the rotation of some part of the earth stopped, and North American and South American plates traveled towards west at the same time (23 hours and 20 minutes) and opposite to the earth's rotational speed,may be equal to rotational speed or less than that. We can calculate the speed of the plates if anybody interested.

We have to find the distance between present ocean ridge in Atlantic under the sea and the length of the ocean bed newly formed from the lithosphere.

The velocity of the plates = Distance traveled/23 hours 20 minutes.

Because of the tremendous velocity of the both plates towards the west the tidal waves traveled towards the east and devastated many places of North Africa, Southern part of present Spain and many civilizations in the Mediterranean region.

Driving Forces of Plate Motion (from Wikipedia and Free Encyclopedia)

"Plate tectonics is a kinematic phenomenon: Earth scientists agree on the observation and deduction that the plates have moved on one another, and debate and find agreements as to how and when. But still, a major question remains as to what the motor behind this movement- the geodynamic mechanism- and here science diverges in different theories."

On earth, this is the common experience of running automobiles with the help of burning fuel and moving a piston inside the engine. We agree that heat moves large vehicles with extremely high speed. We have to believe that God's creation hears creator's voice and the convection currents of earth's interior certainly moves the continents from one place to other whenever it was needed. This was an act of God. The arrogance and greed of Atlantis were punished by God in incredible measure which cannot be understood by human mind.

"Generally, it is accepted that tectonic plates can move because of the relative density of oceanic lithosphere and the relative weakness of the asthenosphere. Dissipation of heat from the mantle is acknowledged to be the source of energy driving plate tectonics, through convection or large-scale upwelling and coming. As a consequence, in the current view, although it is still a matter of some debate, because of the excess density of the oceanic lithosphere sinking in subduction zones a powerful source of plate motion is generated. When the new crust forms at mid-ocean ridges, this oceanic lithosphere is initially less dense than the underlying asthenosphere, but it becomes denser with age, as it conductively cools and thickens. The greater density of old lithosphere about the underlying asthenosphere allows it to sink into the deep mantle at subduction zones, providing most of the driving force for plate motions. The weakness of the asthenosphere allows the tectonic plates to move easily towards a subduction zone. Although subduction is believed to be the strongest force driving plate motions, it cannot be the only force since there are plates such as the North American Plate which are moving, yet are nowhere being subducted. The same is true for the enormous Eurasian Plate. The sources of plate motion are a matter of intensive research and discussion among earth scientists. One of the main points is that the kinematic pattern of the movements itself should be separated clearly from the possible geodynamic mechanism that is invoked as the driving force of the observed movements, as some patterns may be explained by more than one mechanism. The driving forces that are advocated at the moment can be divided into three categories: mantle dynamics related, gravity related (mostly secondary forces), and Earth rotation related."

Why and How the Plates Moved?

(http://www.ucmp.berkeley.edu/education/dynamic/session1/sess1_earthcurrents.html)

"Large convection currents in the asthenosphere transfer heat to the surface, where plumes of less dense magma break apart the plates at the spreading centers, creating divergent plate boundaries.

As the plates move away from the spreading centers, they cool, and the higher density basalt rocks that make up ocean crust get consumed at the ocean trenches/subduction zones. The crust is recycled back into the asthenosphere.

Because ocean plates are denser than continental plates, when these two types of plates converge, the ocean plates are subducted beneath the continental plates. Subduction zones and trenches are convergent margins. The collision of plates is often accompanied by earthquakes and volcanoes."

The findings take a more nuanced shape when we state that the North & South American continents moved westward against and opposite direction to the earth rotation for about a period of 23 hours 20 minutes. As I have mentioned earlier, only above mentioned tectonic plated traveled and the African and Arabian plates stood for about 23 hours 20 minutes. At that terrible day and night the land of Atlantis sunk under the waters of Atlantic. The earth was rotating towards east and the above mentioned plates moved westward minimizing catastrophe and limiting it to the Atlantic and Mediterranean region. It was learned the land of Libya and up to Egypt the catastrophe showed its terrible effect on that region.

The central America people (Aztec) prorated a picture on the stone in their land that dead animals and human beings all other catastrophic rubbish appeared on the shores of central America. The survivors, most probably Mayans, learned that their mother land sunk under the waters.

The geologists may be the right authorities to state pertinently that these movements take millions of years and the plates move few centimeters per year. This is absolutely right today. But during the miracle of Joshua's Long day the speed of the North and South American plates were very high and against the rotation of the earth during 23 hours 20 minutes. Because of the seafloor spreading and the earthquakes taking place on the land of Atlantis, the devastation was terrible and no trace of evidence was found at Azores and the glory of Atlantis was mixed with the lava came out of the junctions of tectonic plates. The latest satellite technology found some evidence of Atlantis in the Atlantic Ocean. Tracing out of the remnant of Atlantis in its glorious state is impossible. But we can see its glory in the ruined state under water.

Rotation Partly Ceased – Revolution of The Earth and Moon Continued

When the author mentioned the stopping of earth's rotation does not signify a stop of the entire earth. But the North American and South American tectonic plates traveled westward on God's command. It was done by lava currents inside the earth. Geologists supports the theory of tectonic plate movements by convection currents inside the earth.

Therefore, the author mentions the rotation of the African and Arabian tectonic plates that ceased for a period of 23 hours and 20minutes in order to give some more time to Joshua for extermination of the Anakim in the Land of Canaan. We must understand that the above said plates traveled against the rotational speed of the earth and opposite to the remaining plates.

At the same time two minor plates Nazca and Cocoos of Pacific region were subducted into the mantle. Some may have attempted a comparison of the present speed of tectonic plates to the speeds activated by convection currents at some point of time in history. The speed of the tectonic plates increased abnormally by God's command on Joshua's Long Day. We cannot compare the momentum of a car in fifth gear on the high way and the speed of a car parking at a certain place. These two plates once moved fast according to the will of God to arrange the continents in its present order.

Here, we should understand that the revolution of earth around sun had not ceased and it continued as it was. If, in case, the earth's revolution stopped there should be a universal devastation in the solar system. Revolution of the earth continued and the earth was safe as the third planet of the solar system. The moon also did not cease to continue its revolution around the earth. If that was happened there was an unthinkable devastation on earth and no one can imagine the extent of this damage or think about Atlantis and anything on the earth. But on God's allowance the African and Arabian tectonic plates ceased to move giving more day light to the Israelites to seek revenge against the giants in those days. Whether the reader agrees or disagrees, the author believes in Creator's authority on the earth and His ability to perform miracles like these which cannot be perceived by man for many thousands of years. The author was not an intelligent person to understand this miracle. But by God's grace he revealed the truth and made available to us. Here, author appreciates every geologist who made incredible work to investigate and their conclusions helped the author to give comfortable solution to the issue of Joshua's Long Day and Atlantis Deluge. Many are still not positive to involve God's hand in human history, for those people this book may be fiction and unscientific. But the author gave every theory that was available today to support the happening of this event which has been shaking the entire earth for many centuries. The act of searching for sugar crystals in melted sugar juice is futile. The Atlantis and its glorious buildings mixed with the lava came out the junctions of tectonic plates and they might have been swallowed by the earth at that time. So some want to see the evidence of the theory proposed. We cannot supply those evidence but only support the geologist's evidence of finding the remains in the Atlantic Ocean. Let us hope that some modern technology can help us to see the buildings mixed with the lava came out of earth in Atlantic Ocean. This incident is real and the Sun standing still was true and the moon stayed in Ajalon was right. May God bless those who can believe this miracle and the omnipotent power of God almighty.

God's acts always have multiple results. The author would like to mention the multiple results of God's intervention in human history:

Answering the prayer of God's servant to provide extra Sun light on that day. Extermination of Anakim on the land of Canaan. Removing the pride and arrogant people, i.e., giants from the land of Atlantis. Rearranging continents for the modern world at safe distances. Removing hindrances against the state of Israelites' in order to send His son Jesus Christ.

Do not misunderstand that God worked in favor of Israelites and punished all other. God showed interest to send His son to this earth as the Abraham's seed because he was the suitable man to be selected by God. It was solely because of his unwavering belief in God. If you wish to believe you will be His favorite. Without faith no one pleases God.

This brings us to the next question: why Minoan and Santorini civilizations were destroyed at the same time?

Many researchers are assuming that the Minoan and Santorini civilizations as Atlantis. But these two places did not match with Plato's story of Atlantis. The Atlantis was existed beyond pillars of Hercules and as big as Asia Minor and Libya together. It is learned that Crete and other Aegean Island, i.e., Santorini flourished from 2500 BC to 1400 BC (approximately).

The Minoan (Crete) civilization destroyed by Thera eruptions. This civilization was destroyed before 3500 years, that is, 1500 BC at the height of the Minoan civilization.

It is said around 1450 BC Minoan culture experienced terrible catastrophes - possibly earthquakes and Thera volcano was the main reason of the downfall of Minoan civilization.

(Quote: Minoan civilization- Wikipedia, the Free Encyclopedia)

“Around 1450 BCE, Minoan culture experienced a turning point due to a natural catastrophe, possibly an earthquake. Another eruption of the Thera volcano has been linked to this downfall, but its dating and implications remain controversial. Several important palaces in locations such as Mallia, Tylissos, Phaistos, Hagia Trade as well as the living quarters of Knossos were destroyed. The palace in Knossos seems to have remained largely intact. This resulted in the Dynasty in Knossos being able to spread its influence over large parts of Crete, until it was overrun by Mycenaean Greeks.”

Many speculated that the Crete or the Santorini were the lost Atlantis? The author is not supporting this argument. It was completely not matching with Plato’s story of Atlantis which existed beyond pillars of Hercules and as big as Asia minor and Libya together. If that was a fact, Plato should have more elaborate explanation about Atlantis, as this was part of Aegean Sea.

(Quote: Destruction of Minoan Civilization, page 140, Explore Crete)

“Somewhere between history and myth lie two historical events of immense importance that shook up and overwhelmed the Hellenic grounds: the destruction of the Minoan Civilization and the eruption of the Santorini volcano, almost 3500 years ago. Since Evans discovered the lost Palace of king Minos in Crete, archaeologists and scientists have been trying to connect the two events.

The predominant theory regarding the destruction of the Minoan Civilization has been –for – years – that it was provoked by something as violent and as sudden as the eruption of Santorini Volcano. Originally it was believed that the eruption took place in 1450 BC, when the Minoan Civilization perished, but newest findings and theories set it somewhere between 1627 BC and 1600 BC."

From the above passages it is noteworthy to observe the time period 1600 BC–1450 BC of their destruction by the catastrophes. Around the above mentioned time period an unusual act of opening of the tectonic plate junctions of Eurasian and African plates as these places were situated in this junction. When the North American Tectonic plate and South American plate moved westward by divergent method, at the junction of the Eurasian, African Tectonic plates, a terrible catastrophe happened in this Mediterranean Sea region.

We find that this process was relatively slow but at These volcanic eruptions were not natural this time of earth opening (tectonic plate opening) there was terrible devastation that had hit the surface of the earth. So there was unavoidable connection between the Atlantis demise and the Thera eruption and Minoan civilization collapse in one day and night.

Plato stated that the devastation taken place in one day and night with terrible earthquakes, fire and tsunamis, these catastrophes was possible only when the tectonic plates moved apart. It is observable that North American and South American tectonic plates were divergent plates and present oceanic bed as formed only at 1500 BC. This issue opens up newer avenues for research. The present ocean bed was a part of earth mantle in liquid form and it came out as layer when God Commands for that. The author believes that whenever it is necessary to God He sends the outer layers into mantle and whenever it needed new layers comes out as divergent plates. The convergent plates went inside the earth or slipped under another plate to melt as in the Blast furnace of steel plant.

Azores Was the Remnant of Atlantis!

All the islands of Azores were the remnant of ancient Atlantis. This also perfectly fit with the Plato story of Atlantis and also it is situated at the junction of North, South and African and Eurasian tectonic plates. Azores were the mountain peaks of this drowned island. The Atlantis was torn and rent by tremendous volcanic convulsions, earthquakes and it descended into the Ocean as the South and North American plates traveled westward in that terrible day and night. Now we found great strata of lava with whole face of the sunken land covered for thousands of miles with volcanic remnant which furnished the necessary proof of the truth of Plato's statement "in one day and one fatal night there came mighty earthquakes and inundations which in gulfed that mighty people of Atlantis." There were no such earthquakes in the recorded history of earth. This incident was unique and God heard prayers of Joshua and stopped earth's rotation partly by the command of God. A race has to be started on the earth to send His beloved son Jesus Christ.

Atlantis disappeared beneath the sea; and now that sea became inaccessible on the account of the quantity of mud and lava. It was not possible to dig the glory of Atlantis under water. Now, this being mixed with hot lava that came from the tectonic plate junctions, the constructions broke down and buried under the enormous amount of lava came out from the earth's asthenoshpere.

At the turn of the thirteenth century the earth suffered some disturbances due to the tectonic plate movements.

According to Plato, the priests of Sais told that at the time Atlantis great fires destroyed many lands and forests, earthquakes shook the world and wrought enormous destruction, many springs and rivers dried up (on African and Eurasian tectonic plates). Finally, great floods and rainstorms added to the chaos. This type of devastation possible only when the tectonic plates moved on the earth. So we can conclude that the Azores islands in Atlantic Ocean were the remnant of ancient Atlantis.

Bible says everything on earth was created for Jesus and through Him. So the ultimate plan of God is sending His son to this perverted world. We can observe that no Nephilim found in anywhere after the incarnation of Jesus Christ on this earth.

Conclusion

The Atlantis disappeared @ Joshua's Long Day. This was an act of God. It was a great miracle (in man's perceptive) that occurred to hear the prayers of his faithful servant Joshua. God intended to eradicate another batch of Nephilim from the face of the earth, because He saw people turn greedy and arrogant subduing the surrounding kingdoms to spread their belief system. In order to punish the arrogant Atlanteans and to establish a new race on the earth for sending His son Jesus Christ, God allowed this incident on earth. Satan tried to pollute the minds of God's followers as the thoughts of Nephlim were evil (Genesis 6:5). The enemy tried to pollute the human race so that the Messiah would not come to this earth. The Almighty God took severe action to stop this, and also the time of establishing a kingdom for His people and to give His laws and commandments has arrived.

Here one thing we have to remember that David was honored as the forefather of Jesus Christ because he and his soldiers killed the last remnant of the Anakim. They killed Goliath and his brothers. Last giant on earth was killed by King David. So God favored David and sent His only begotten son to this world as Son of David. Satan tried to spoil the purity of the human race, Jesus re-established this divine purity through Jacob at the river Jabbok (Genesis32:22-28). Jacob became the father of the nation Israel.

Everything is possible with God. It may be hard to grasp this miracle of God. Many may raise doubts on how these plates which weigh millions of trillions of tones move such a long distance in one day and night. We know that man is moving many tones of weight by burning the fuel in a closed container. All the automobiles were working on this principle of burning and piston moving. We know that the inner earth was full of burning rock liquids of lava and the scientists found that these lava currents were moving in circles. By God's command the tectonic plates inside the earth and sometimes the liquid lava comes out as a new layer to the earth (please refer some sites regarding Tectonic plate movements in internet). If you believe the Biblical Creation, God made the layers come together to shown up the dryland in one day, i.e., third day of the creation (Genesis 1: 9-13). How did waters came together into one place? The water always flows downwards. So the earth layers' traveled from different directions so that the waters were gathered together. This was done by God in one day. Now shall we dare to believe that God made the North and South American plates moved westward in 23 hours and 20 minutes! There is wide scope to investigate how the mountain range formed in the western shores of North and South American continents and why the volcanic activity was active in a larger scale. These mountain ranges may also have formed during the Atlantis Deluge. Investigation and research should confirm this issue.

The geologists found many similarities between the pyramids of Mexico, Central America and Peruvian culture. Mayan culture continued in Mexico. The author believes that the parent culture for all these were Atlantis as central American region was at navigable distance before the deluge of Atlantis. It was proven that Mayan people propagated false doctrines and ideas and they prepared calendars to fix a date for the end of the World. We are all knew that was a hoax on 21 Dec, 2012. Why because the evil spirits behind the Atlanteans encouraged to bring out wrong ideas towards future. The same thing was learned by Mayans. Moreover, the people of Atlantis practiced king's worship by offering sacrifices to the Kings of the land. They arrogantly subdued the surrounding people and forced them to follow their traditions. They tried to bring all other tribes into their fold by force with greediness at its peak in those days. They tried to win the Athenian people but they fought against them and driven then beyond the pillars of Hercules. This point is yet another evidence that Atlantis was situated against the pillars of Hercules and not anywhere else.

Knowingly or unknowingly we do not know, these people occupied a continent which was formed mainly by volcanic activity and most importantly at the junctions of three tectonic plates which the author mentioned earlier. This was also their fate to be wiped out from the earth.

By all these evidences and references the continent of Atlantis was real and its deluge in Atlantic Ocean also a fact. But Plato's time of Atlantis demise was not correct. From the above facts mentioned in this book gives you clarity that Joshua's Long Day was at the rate of American Tectonic Plates or we can say Atlantis Demise@ Joshua's Long day.

Joshua's Long Day was commanded by God and the way it happened will always remain a dark mystery. This mystery was revealed by God through Holy Spirit in these days which would not have been possible if the discoveries about earth structure and tectonic plate movements were not available. The author arrived at a comfortable solution to this problem by going through the researches and historical findings of the scientists and geologists.

The key phrase of this book is 'Atlantis Deluge in one day and night.' When we observe the geological history of the earth, there was no evidence of such catastrophes in modern society except the demise of Atlantis in ancient days. So the author has rightfully and authentically concluded that there was a link between Joshua's Long Day and Atlantis demise. When the author searched for the date of Atlantis demise the date proposed by Plato was seemed to be wrong reckoning. 9500 years before Plato was not comfortable to be think about an advanced society of Atlantis. Hence, the Atlantis society belongs to Bronze age period which was between 3500 BC–1200 BC. So this period was the comfortable period of Atlantis flourishing and demise. The devastations occurred in and around Mediterranean Sea supports our claim of Atlantis deluge at 1405 BC which well fitted with the date of Joshua's Long Day.

In order to understand the North and South American plate movements we have to think in more multiple way that while earth was rotating eastward, suddenly the above mentioned Tectonic plates start traveling towards west with opposite direction to the rotation of the earth to reach present positions in a single day and night.

In fact, this opposite and against the rotation of the earth the devastation was minimized in this region. Even this minimized effect of the earthquakes and Tsunamis devastated the land of Atlantis and the places in Mediterranean Sea, the western shores of North Africa and southern shores of Europe at that time. One thing I wish to tell that the Earth's revolving around the Sun never ceased. Moon also did not stop to revolve round the earth at that time. The mysteries belong to Lord, the God.

"The secrets things belong unto the LORD our God: but those things which are revealed belong forever, that we may do all the words of this law." (Deu 29:29).

To rest the case, author's conclusion is that Atlantis Demise @ Joshua's Long Day. May God enlighten and bless every reader of this book abundantly.

In case any difficulty to understand this book the author is willing to come to your place to explain further with the help of pictures and a globe. Thank you!

Photo Gallery

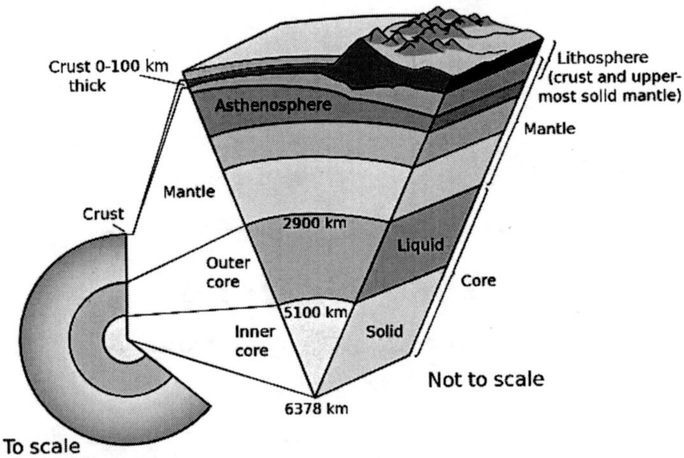

Layers of the Earth & Earth's interior structure

Atlas who bearing a sphere

Map showing Atlantis in Atlantic Ocean with plate junctions.

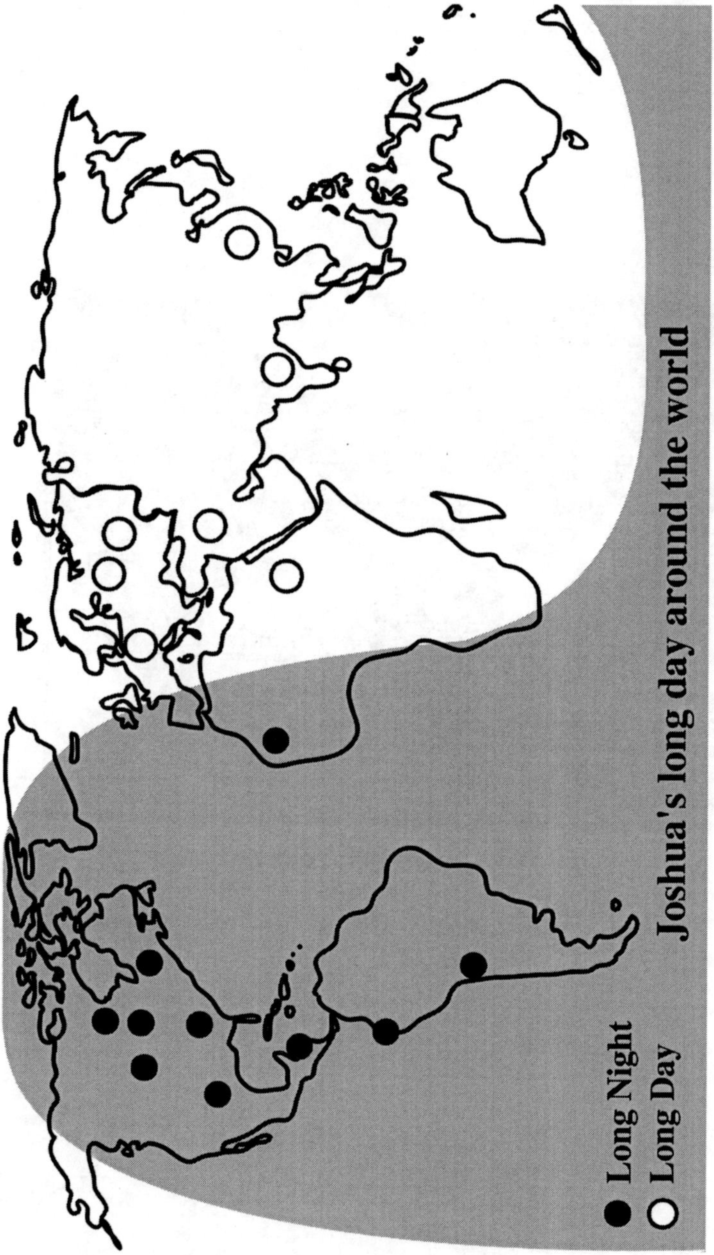
Joshua's long day around the world
● Long Night
○ Long Day

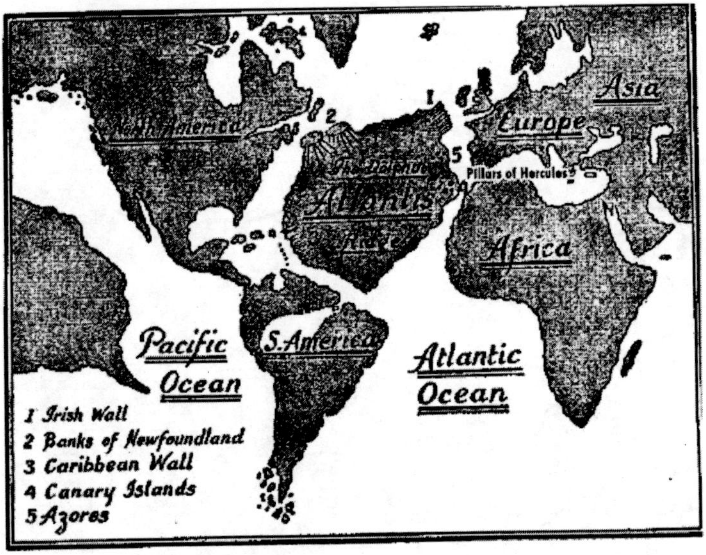

Atlantics against Pillars of Hercules

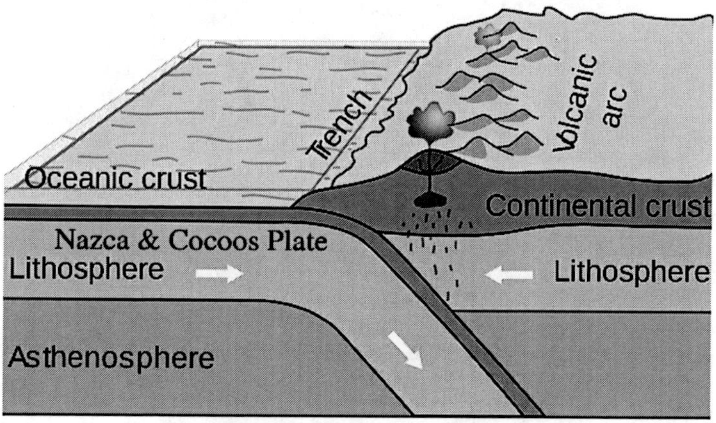

Subduction and Volcanic activity - Seafloor spreading

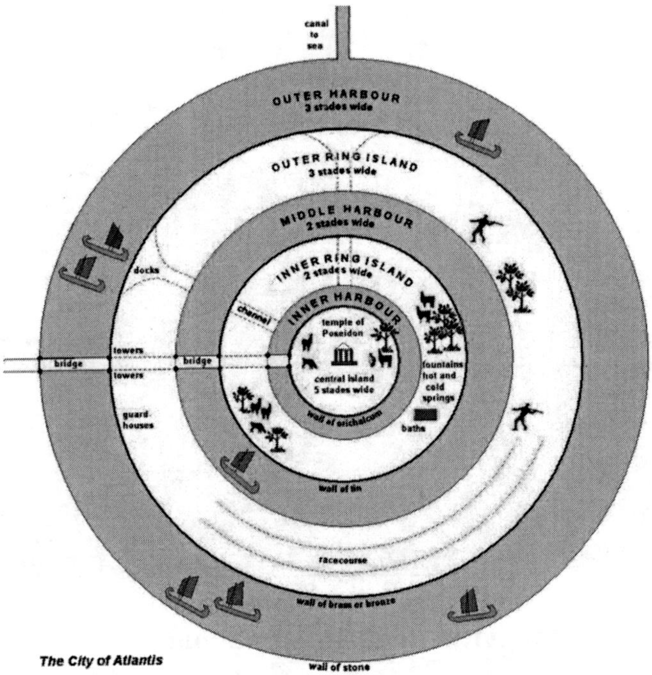

Rings of ancient Atlantis

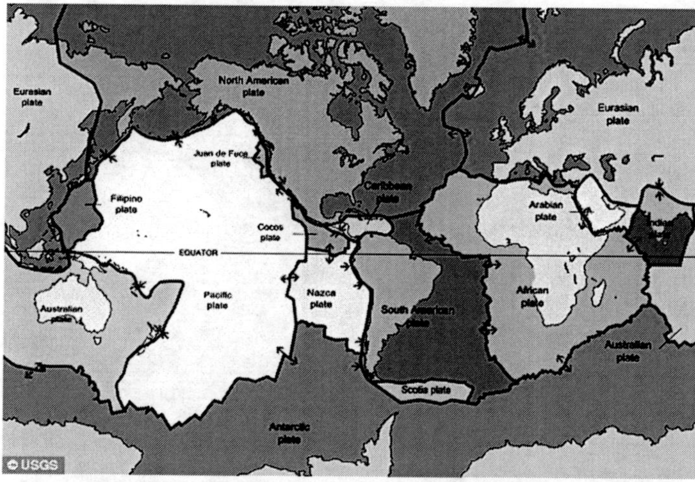

Tectonic plate divisions of the Earth

North & South American plate boundaries after the Deluge

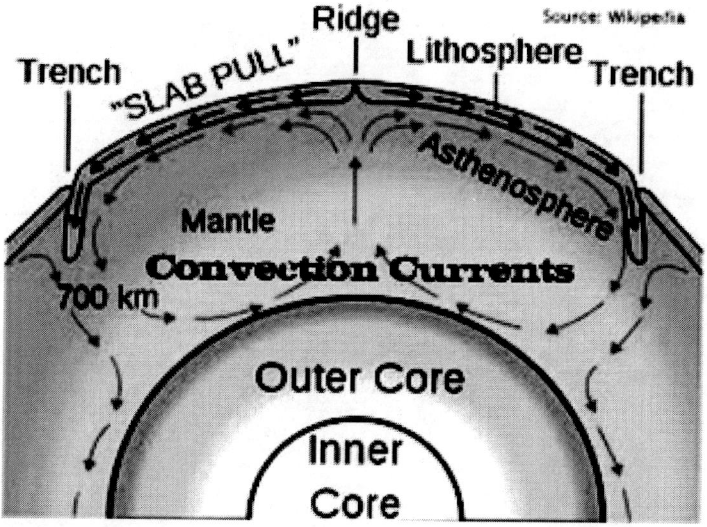

Convection Currents of the Lava in the Mantle

Bibliography:

1. Holy Bible (NIV, KJV, ESV and NKJV)
2. Dr.Micheal Eaton, Preaching through the Bible, Genesis 1-11
3. Jurgen Spanuth, Atlantis - The mystery Unraveled
4. Frank Joseph, Atlantis Encyclopedia
5. Zechariah Sitchin, America's First civilization
6. John Antonopolus, The great Minoan eruption of Thera volcano and ensuing Tsunami in the greek Archipelago
7. Website: Cherubini_et_al ANTIQUITY_2014.pdf
8. Walter L. Freidrick, The Minoan eruption of Santorini around 1613 BC and its consequences.
9. Language of God - in History - Watchers (chapter - 4)
10. Website: got questions.org - who were the Anakim & Does Bible mention the lost city of Atlantis
11. Harry Rimmer - Joshua's Long Day.pdf
12. Henry David Thoreau- Structure of the Earth.
13. Jes Alexander, Abstracting Atlantis
14. Harold Hill, Joshua's Missing Day Story
15. Website: www.ucmp.berkely.edu
16. Destruction of Minoan Civilization, Explore Crete
17. Free Wikipedia, Encyclopedia.

Other books by the same author

1. Anthyadinamulu @ Mruthasamudramu

In the Holy Bible there are many mysteries which are beyond human comprehension. However, it is worth unraveling these mysteries surrounding the prophesies uttered by Lord Jesus Christ. One of such prophesies is found in Mathew 24:28 and Luke 17:37 respectively.

"For wheresoever the carcass is, there will the eagles be gathered together"(KJV)

"And they answered and said unto him, Where, Lord? And he said unto them, whosesoever the body is, thither will the eagles be gathered together"(KJV)

So Jesus Christ used this as a special statement to explain the severity of the end-time events to all mankind as well as Israel. That is why Lord used the words 'carcass' and 'eagles.' Then immediately I connected them to Dead Sea and its history.

Here the words 'thither' 'there' reveal about a particular place or region. This region is a place where the disobedient people of Sodom and gomarrow were burnt alive by fire and brimstone. That region is called 'Dead Sea' in the present times it will become a focal point for the end-time events.

The revelation of this mystery, hidden in the prophetic verses given above was revealed to me through personal enlightenment by the Holy Spirit. This book was written with such a spirit and not with human wisdom. I am looking forward to publish this book, “End-Times @ Dead Sea” in order to make it available to every Christian.

Note: This book has to be published in English. Anyone interested to publish it please contact the author

While translating the above book the word ‘carcass’ led me to find the actual location of Garden of Eden on the face of the earth. So I have authored another title in English ‘Paradise Found’

2. Paradise Found

The Paradise ‘Garden of Eden’ was lost due to the sin and disobedience of the first Adam. This was a big loss to the entire human race. This Paradise went missing from the earth and history. This was a hidden mystery from the beginning. There is an answer for every problem in the Bible. Where was the Garden of Eden? This was the challenging issue to every Christian and non-Christian. The prominent 17th century poet narrated the story of ‘Paradise Lost’ through his poetry. But we do not know actual location of this Paradise.

God revealed the mystery to his servant and the Paradise was Found in Israel itself. Do you wish to know the location of the “Garden of Eden” on the face of the earth? Please join me by reading the truth which God revealed about the lost Paradise which was the Garden of Eden, then you can find it on earth geographically and also agree with me. Praise the Lord, the Paradise was found. Those who lost the Paradise in their hearts should read this book diligently, so that the Spirit of God can be restored.

“But thou art cast forth away from thy sepulcher like an abominable branch, clothed with the slain, that are thrust through with the sword, that go down to the stones of the pit; as a dead body trodden under foot." Isaiah 14:19 (ASV).

It is available in Amazon.com - Paradise Found by Anipe Steeven Premajothi.

Author's Family

Sumanth, Hemanth, Rev. A. Steeven Premajyothi, Vijayakumari, Theressa